for Will,
in warm recognition of,
and gratitude for,
our TLS friendship,

Patrick, Elsworth, 10 September
2024.

Wagner's Theatre

Wagner's Theatre

In Search of a Legacy

Patrick Carnegy

with an introduction by John Deathridge

The Lutterworth Press

THE LUTTERWORTH PRESS
P.O. Box 60
Cambridge
CB1 2NT
United Kingdom
www.lutterworth.com
publishing@lutterworth.com

Hardback ISBN: 978 0 7188 9743 7
Paperback ISBN: 978 0 7188 9740 6
PDF ISBN: 978 0 7188 9741 3
ePub ISBN: 978 0 7188 9742 0

British Library Cataloguing in Publication Data
A record is available from the British Library

First published by The Lutterworth Press 2024

Imagine yourself entering into the spaces of a communal theatre of the future and you'd see without even trying how open they are to an unimaginably rich array of new ideas.

—Richard Wagner, 'The Artwork of the Future', 1850

For my cousin and inspirational first mentor
Dr Graeme Tytler
on his 90th Birthday

Contents

Introduction

Can we ever have a sensible conversation about opera? The question is still present in Patrick Carnegy's engaging new book, which I am honoured to introduce here. The book is not quite what it seems to be at first sight. Under its beautiful surface are signs of turmoil in the opera world in general and among Wagner's interpreters in particular, especially the attempts of Wieland Wagner, Joachim Herz, Patrice Chéreau and Hans-Jürgen Syberberg to reinterpret him after Hitler. Wagner created many of these turbulences himself, including issues about funding models and a sophisticated idea of performance that demanded controversial and constant reinvention, not just of his own works, but of beloved composers and operas as well. (His re-orchestrations of Beethoven and radical reworking of Gluck's *Iphigénie en Aulide* for which he even changed the ending, are two good examples.) Now we have seven successful Amazon television series in 40 chapters about the trials and tribulations of classical music in New York collectively called *Mozart in the Jungle*, I don't see why there shouldn't be a *Wagner in the Jungle* to follow. A clip from Steven Spielberg's *Jurassic Park* might be a good start: those two glasses of water with barely noticeable ripples for instance that grow ominously wider as the footfall of a big beast makes itself felt. In this book too there is a subtle crescendo of very real crises, aesthetic and political, as we progress.

Since the 1960s Patrick Carnegy has been a keen observer in the jungle. A music critic for *The Times* and *The Observer*, assistant editor at *The Times Literary Supplement*, music-books editor at Faber & Faber where he published writings by Mahler, Schoenberg and Stravinsky, a key position in the managerial framework of the Royal Opera House, and then fifteen years as *The Spectator*'s Stratford-upon-Avon drama critic, during which he wrote some 120 shrewdly observed reviews about Shakespeare performance. If jungles had ringside seats as they do in cinemas, I imagine that Patrick must have always been sitting in the very front row.

Reading his pioneer work on Wagner production – a big gap in theatre history until he published his masterpiece *Wagner and the Art of the Theatre* (2006) after years of painstaking research – there is a sense that Patrick was there at performances in the past as well. Reporting on the immediate sense of vastly different takes on Wagner's stage works wherever they took place, the way they looked, how singers moved, directors directed, the smell of the times that influenced the way they were judged, he takes us through a veritable cornucopia of detail about Wagner in action. We witness Wagner doing the things he liked best, composing works for the stage, directing, and in his younger years conducting them. And we get very close to others in history reinterpreting them for the theatre, so close in fact that we almost feel the grease paint and the impact of the *mise-en-scène*. Wagner wrote to Ludwig II just before the premiere of *Tristan und Isolde* in 1865 that his work is 'only complete when as drama it fully and physically comes to life in front of us and speaks directly to our hearts and senses'. It was a condition for all his works, for all their future interpreters, and for all who wanted to write about them. As Patrick was one of the first to show at length, the staging of a Wagner work is crucial and anyone who would claim to have fully grasped Wagner's achievement cannot afford to ignore it.

About *Wagner and the Art of the Theatre*, Pierre Boulez said at the time of its appearance that he truly believed it to be 'one of the best documented publications in all the recent literature on Wagner'. It still is. With even richer documentation, a third of it this time in colour, this new book ventures into broader ramifications of Wagner's legacy, including a detailed account of mind-blowing productions like *Tristan und Isolde* in 1903 Vienna conducted by Mahler with Alfred Roller as scenic director. It was a landmark in theatre history, rightly seen here as the moment when producers of opera not only broke decisively with the absurd literalism and only-according-to-the-master's-voice authoritarianism of Bayreuth, but also finally established the idea that producers are perfectly within their rights radically to reconceive works of art against the grain of what their creators originally wanted – or rather what some members of audiences think they wanted – much as Wagner himself did with Beethoven and Gluck. Influenced by the Vienna Secession at the turn of the century, 'director's theatre' (*Regietheater*) was essentially born. And so was the controversy that has accompanied it ever since.

The book opens with a previously unpublished essay on the absorption of Shakespeare into Wagner's own ideas about drama. Again, it is a pioneering study. A larger historical and critical question that has never been adequately answered convincingly is how Shakespeare was injected creatively into the cultural bloodstream of German-speaking theatre in the eighteenth and nineteenth centuries. German-speaking literary figures had a tendency to see Shakespeare as one of their own, frequently praising August Wilhelm Schlegel's famous translations (by the time we get to the nineteenth century when they were augmented by translations by Wolf Baudissin and Dorothea and Ludwig Tieck) as superior to the original. The haughty judgement obviously begs the question of how well the distinguished German-speaking champions of the English Bard, including Wagner, understood the plays if they referred to them, as they often did with only half-joking smiles, in their 'English version', in contrast to what was felt to be the true home they had found in the German language. Perhaps in retaliation English-speaking critics have tended to describe Shakespeare's influence on Wagner as minor. Here in Patrick's foray into the subject we realize just how wide of the mark that is. Simply put, Wagner would not have spent as much time as he did from his youth through middle age to his last years reading, discussing, writing about Shakespeare and attending performances of the plays if all of that had not been of central importance to his art. Taking major stretches of the *Ring* as just one instance, the pathways of suffering and undaunted representations of violence, not to mention the ethical mayhem strewn over the cycle's tragic journey, owe a great deal to Shakespeare's example.

The next five chapters are devoted to productions over a span of a hundred years from the premiere of the *Ring* in 1876, under Wagner's own direction, to the centennial production by Patrice Chéreau conducted by Pierre Boulez. As is well known, the latter has been greeted in some circles with storms of abuse. For many Wagner enthusiasts and philosophers passionately interested in Wagner, the ideas of Chéreau and Boulez were a centennial bridge too far. The complainers felt cheated because the two pesky Frenchman had robbed the *Ring* of its totalizing mythology in full dress, so to speak, and its supposed romantic inheritance, despite Wagner's insistence time and again that with the *Ring* he had made a decisive break with romanticism. This so-called French *Ring* was no longer a mystifying exercise in comforting profundities about human life seen through the gauze of remote myth or lazy symbolism, but a tour de force of intense, emotionally involved acting (clichéd operatic gestures were banned) and a provocative mixture of mythic and modern imagery in the director's imagination that brought audiences into closer touch with violence, remorse and suicidal suffering. Even its playful elements were a painful counterpoint to the overall melancholy of the story. It felt uncomfortably close to the world we live in ('life as it really is', as Wagner said when talking in private about his amazing conception), and probably for this simple reason, despite the protests of a minority, it eventually met with great success. Patrick is refreshingly frank about his own mixed feelings about the centennial *Ring*. Apart from the tiny fistful of philosophers, however, more significant in the context of the documentary wealth of his research is the large brigade of serious Wagner watchers who clamoured for a return to Wagner's original intentions. Little did they know then, though they will if they read this book, just how fragmentary the historical record actually is. Patrick relishes the recent discovery of the diaries of Alfred Pringsheim, a noted professor of mathematics who recorded some fascinating critical observations while visiting the rehearsals and performances of the 1876 Bayreuth Festival, but regrets that a third of them are lost. We have no photographs of what the staging looked like (those of the singers were done in photographers' studios) and there is no guarantee that Josef Hoffmann's paintings of his scenic designs commissioned by Wagner looked like the scenery that was eventually built. Everywhere the records of what happened in the making and performance of the production are frustratingly incomplete.

A large part of this book is devoted to highly readable reviews of books about a 'quartet' of conductors: Toscanini, Klemperer, Karajan, Solti. Patrick casts his critical eye over these figures and the attempts of their biographers to capture – not always with total success – their extraordinary careers. The implicit link is that they all flourished in the tradition of the conductor-as-interpreter (as opposed to the mere time-beater) that emerged from the nineteenth century into the twentieth with the massive authority of Wagner behind it. Wagner was not the only one to establish the role of conductors as high-octane celebrities who match – even sometimes out-match – the genius of the composers whose works they bring back to life. But in the 1830s and early 1840s as an ambitious twenty-something composer and Musikdirektor striving for international recognition, he was already fashioning the idea of himself in concerts and opera houses as the visible conduit of great music (Beethoven and Weber especially), which in the long run would lend historical legitimacy to his own work and the 'master' conductor capable of conveying its message. If we add Mahler, who is prominent in the earlier chapter on Roller's *Tristan*, it is striking that three of the five conductors Patrick writes about – Mahler, Klemperer, Solti – were Jewish. All three had to make their peace with Wagner's anti-Semitism. Wagner's practical and philosophical view of the conductor's role, which he set out in his treatise *On Conducting* (published in 1869, the same year as the expanded version of his polemic *Judaism in Music*), was coloured by a deliberately controversial distinction between German Jewish conductors, who supposedly skim efficiently through Beethoven without dwelling strongly on anything too profound, and those who are 'properly' German and hence able to catch fire and penetrate the sublime depths of German music in a way their Jewish brethren never could. *On Conducting* was a highly influential document for generations of conductors. Over the years, many who were Jewish took note along with everyone else of Wagner's ideas about variable tempi, phrasing, how to conduct specific works by Mozart, Beethoven and Weber, and why the conductor has huge potential as an interpreter. But not a few Jewish conductors like Mahler, Klemperer and Solti also turned out to be truly outstanding interpreters with wide repertoires, including Wagner. This could be an instance of Wagner's legacy saving him from the worst of himself. As time passed, the fact that generations of Jewish conductors contributed in major ways to his legacy has been proof that his original prejudice was complete nonsense, eminently forgettable, even though it undeniably left behind eerie echoes in the notorious Nazi attempts to erase Jewish conductors and composers for ever from Germany's cultural map. For that reason alone it is still not easy to forgive.

The last part of the book is an offshoot from Patrick's experience working for the Royal Opera House in the late 1980s and early 1990s. What he wrote in the light of opera's crises just a few years later still feels for me acutely relevant now. Indeed, only three weeks before starting this introduction I heard about the decision of the Arts Council of England (ACE) on 4 November 2022 to scale down financial support for four major opera companies in the UK. That included the cancellation of the entire annual recurring grant for English National Opera (ENO) at the London Coliseum, one of Britain's most important venues for opera. In a matter of months after 130 years of remarkable history, ENO's extinction, as I write, is on the cards. (If it still exists when you read this, it will be a miracle.)

Included in this final section is a scorching review of two books by former bosses of the Royal Opera House with decidedly different opinions about what opera can do and how it should be managed. Their views are basically antagonistic. But on one thing they agree: 'that the House has always been strapped for cash'. We are back in the jungle. The climax arrives in Patrick's next, and highly perceptive, review of Suzie Gilbert's 2009 book *Opera for Everybody: The Story of English National Opera*, which in part is also the story of the huge financial deficit incurred by that institution during its most adventurous years. The title of the review, 'Blood on the Carpet', says it all. It reverberated widely then. And now, because of ACE's blunder more than a decade later, the beast is closer and louder than ever. ACE's director of music thinks that 'traditionally staged "grand" or large-scale opera' has shown 'almost no growth in audience demand'. Behold, the heavy footfall of lazy ACE-speak, this time coyly standing in for all the old prejudices.

Why opera at all? Is it 'relevant'? Why the vast sums – especially taxpayers' money – wasted on the yearly resurrection and preservation of an art form that's supposedly little more than decadent?

It's an old story. Wagner was already railing against the beast in 1848 when, after elections in Saxony of radical revolutionary-minded delegates, the subvention of the Court Theatre in Dresden was to be cut because it was merely a luxurious place of entertainment. His response was a detailed proposal for theatre reform running to 45 closely printed pages, brimming with new ideas about an interaction of all the arts that could restore 'true dignity' ('wahre Würde') to theatre. He was not the first or the last. In 1790, when French revolutionaries were questioning opera's connections to the old regime, Beaumarchais wrote in a preface to his libretto for *Tarare* (music by Salieri) that to survive opera should get serious about drama. And Brecht, no less adamant in the economic crisis of 1930 when state exchequers in Germany's Weimar Republic questioned opera's 'relevance' as an excuse to balance their beleaguered budgets, responded with two highly original operas with Kurt Weill and a lament that 'nobody demands a fundamental discussion of opera (its function!)'. As Patrick points out here in his absorbing review of Peter Heyworth's biography of the conductor Otto Klemperer, Berlin's Kroll Opera was peremptorily closed down for 'economic' reasons only a year after Brecht made his remarks. Since 1927 it had been demonstrating – with deeds rather than words – how new conversations about opera production for contemporary audiences can bear precious fruit. But nobody in power was listening. Patrick's own book surely makes an important contribution to the issue by reminding us that history shows us just how much danger opera is in if a productive conversation about it is forced to stop.

Appropriately enough, the book ends with an actual conversation about opera. Sir Michael Tippett was a profoundly humane British composer with almost Homeric ambitions for opera and its still far from exhausted possibilities. Not everyone will agree he won all his battles. But this exchange with Patrick, with Wagner looking over his shoulder at key moments, is a heroic effort to explore what serious opera is capable of achieving, even in these days when it feels more challenged than it ever has been before. Thank you, Patrick, for letting us read it again.

John Deathridge
Emeritus King Edward Professor of Music
King's College London
3 January 2023

Prelude

These pages are a testament to my experience of half a century of landmark stagings of Wagner's operas.

My first visit to Bayreuth in 1967, as music critic for *The Times*, inspired a lifetime's interest in Wagner and especially in the stage history of his works. As a critic I have had the good fortune to have seen and written about most of the important productions of his operas in the latter half of the twentieth century, nearly all of them controversial at first and subsequently regarded as classics. My 2006 book, *Wagner and the Art of the Theatre*, was an attempt to place these productions in their historical context and to discuss why they represented such a radical break with tradition.

Some of the pieces in this new book explore the themes of *Wagner and the Art of the Theatre* in greater depth, but they also respond to recent discoveries, as of Thomas Mann's father-in-law's eye-witness account of rehearsals for the *Ring*'s Bayreuth premiere in 1876, and of long-lost scenic designs for it.

Much of the book is indebted to my experiences as the first-ever dramaturg (literary and production adviser) to be appointed at Covent Garden (1988-92). It was not an easy task, as my accounts of the backstage workings of the Royal Opera House and, with less authority, of English National Opera at troubled points in their history will surely reveal.

In our time the staging not only of Wagner but also of opera in general has become a hot and controversial topic, largely through directors whose radical productions, sometimes described as *Regietheater* (director's theatre), have been seen as betrayals of the composer's intentions. This has opened up a raging debate to which I hope this book will contribute.

But it seems wisest to begin on less controversial territory by remarking on Shakespeare's largely unsung influence on Wagner and in particular on *Die Meistersinger*, an influence echoed in a famous Bayreuth production by the composer's grandson, Wieland. I go on to describe the revelatory account by Thomas Mann's father-in-law, Alfred Pringsheim, of the rehearsals for the *Ring*'s 1876 Bayreuth premiere, a text that remained unknown until 2013. I then discuss how our impressions of the cinematic visual world Wagner envisioned have been enhanced by the discovery of the original coloured versions of the artist Josef Hoffmann's designs, previously known only in monochrome.

After Wagner, of course, everything has been called into question. I explore seismic theatrical moments – beginning with Gustav Mahler and Alfred Roller's radical reinvention of the Wagnerian stage. Hitler's adulation of the composer famously cast a long and deeply uncomfortable shadow over Bayreuth, and indeed more widely. I show how after the war West- and East-German directors sought, in diametrically opposed ways, to exorcise the demons, on the one hand by attempting to de-politicize Wagner, and on the other by re-politicizing him in the direction of Marxist socialism. Their productions, together with Patrice Chéreau and Pierre Boulez's iconoclastic centenary *Ring* at Bayreuth, and Hans-Jürgen Syberberg's inquisitorial 1982 film of *Parsifal*, have permanently changed our post-war understanding of Wagner and the course of virtually all subsequent interpretations of his work.

Toscanini, Klemperer, Karajan and Solti, the four great Wagnerian conductors whom I discuss next, experienced remarkably different problems with these demons. Toscanini rebuffed Hitler in 1933 by pulling out of his Bayreuth commitment, throwing his international fame behind the struggle against fascism. Klemperer, convinced that the world that dawned in 1918 was one 'in opposition to Wagner', nevertheless staged at the Berlin Kroll Opera in 1929 a demythologized *Der fliegende Holländer* that 'mobilized a reserve of actuality in Wagner … which will explode today or tomorrow' (T.W. Adorno) – which it did indeed in the 1976 Chéreau *Ring*. With Karajan the musical politics become uncomfortably murky, but also rich in paradox. Membership of the Nazi Party had been a price for his meteoric rise in the 1930s, yet Hitler dismissed his Wagner as 'insufficiently German'.

As a 33-year-old, the Hungarian Solti electrified the discredited German opera scene in the aftermath of the war, belatedly making his Bayreuth debut in the Peter Hall *Ring* of 1983. But he should best be remembered for the energy and emotional power of Decca's first-ever studio recording (1958-65) of the complete tetralogy, with George London and Hans Hotter as Wotan, Birgit Nilsson as Brünnhilde and Wolfgang Windgassen as Siegfried. As music director of Covent Garden ('The Royal Opera' from 1968) he raised its standing to the highest international level.

Like Wagner, Sir Michael Tippett wrote both the words and music of his operas and thought deeply about the possibilities of musical drama. The book concludes with my 1977 conversation with Sir Michael about his own operas, and opera in general. It is frequently quoted but has never been reprinted since its first publication in *The Times Literary Supplement* (*TLS*).

Two of my essays are published here for the first time. The others began life as reviews of performances and books, or were originally given as lectures, their sources being detailed at the end of each piece. Translations, unless otherwise acknowledged, are my own.

I gratefully acknowledge my huge debt to John Gross, editor of the *TLS* (1974-81) and dear friend, who gave me the freedom to write at length about books and performances, and to the present editor, Martin Ivens, for permission to reprint some of these articles. My thanks no less to Barry Millington, founding editor of *The Wagner Journal*, beacon of intelligent writing about theatrical performance, for his collegiate friendship over many years, and for permission to reprint two of my pieces. My similar thanks for reprint permission to the University Press of America, Libreria Musicale

Italiana (Lucca), *Wagner News*, Cambridge University Press and the *The London Review of Books*. I am grateful to Kate Hopkins and Christopher Wintle for their editorial assistance at an earlier stage of planning this book.

It has been a sustaining pleasure to have worked with Adrian Brink, Sarah Algar-Hughes, Georgina Melia and their colleagues at Lutterworth Press. For help with the illustrations I am much indebted to Evan Baker and to Christopher Halls for his photography. Wagner's great-granddaughter Dagny Beidler and the Mariann Steegmann Foundation have generously supported the costs of including the enchanting watercolours by the composer's 15-year-old daughter, Isolde. Cornelia von Bodenhausen kindly gave permission for the reproduction of the Josef Hoffmann *Ring* paintings in her collection and these were specially photographed by Sophie Dewulf.

For her insight and encouragement over so many years, my warmest thanks are to my wife, Jill Gomez.

Patrick Carnegy

Cambridge, 2024

Part One

The Master's Dream

Illustration 1: 'Aeschylus and Shakespeare, who according to [Heinrich] Porges, are the only two dramatists with whom Wagner can be compared, pay homage to the Master in their historically correct dress', caption to an 1876 cartoon from the time of the first complete performance of the *Ring* at Bayreuth.

Chapter One

Wagner and his Shakespeare[1]

Wagner was never shy to acknowledge his indebtedness to Aeschylus and Shakespeare, seeing himself as their heir and a dramatist of comparable, if not superior, stature – a claim that did not escape the attention of a contemporary cartoonist.

It is of course the Aeschylean influence, and that of the Greek tragedians as whole, that has attracted most attention, as from Wolfgang Schadewaldt, Hugh Lloyd-Jones, Michael Ewans, Simon Goldhill, Daniel H. Foster and many others.[2] But Wagner was

---

1. Source: Unpublished talk given at Trinity Hall, Cambridge, 28 October 2013; for the London Wagner Society, 10 September 2015; and in the Jubilee Hall, Aldeburgh, 23 September 2016.

2. From the extensive bibliography, I mention a mere handful of titles: Wolfgang Schadewaldt, 'Richard Wagner und die Griechen', three articles in the *Bayreuther Programmhefte*, 1962-64; a translation of the first article by David C. Durst, with a commentary by John Deathridge, in *Dialogos (Hellenic Studies Review)*, no. 6 (1999); Hugh Lloyd-Jones, *Blood for the Ghosts* (London: Duckworth, 1982); Michael Ewans, *Wagner and Aeschylus: The 'Ring' and the 'Oresteia'* (London: Faber, 1982); Simon Goldhill, 'Wagner and the Greeks'

stunningly well read across the spectrum of Western literature. Along with the Greek dramatists his favourite authors included Calderón, Lope de Vega, Goethe, Lessing, Schiller, E.T.A. Hoffmann – and, especially, Shakespeare. I will try to suggest that the Shakespearean influence has been unjustly overlooked,[3] and will conclude by discussing three outstanding post-war stagings of *Die Meistersinger von Nürnberg* that were Shakespearean in character.

Yes, Shakespeare was a dramatist, not a composer. But for Wagner, it was always drama, intensified through and in *music*, that was his goal. Not 'opera' in any Italian or French sense, but German music-drama, an apotheosis of every dramatic form known to him. And it was to Shakespeare's plays, which he knew inside out, that he returned more often than to any other inspirational source.

A theatrical apprenticeship

Richard Wagner, ninth child of his parents, was born on 22 May 1813 in Leipzig in the old inn *Zum Roten und Weißen Löwen* (The Red and White Lion). He could scarcely have been born into a more theatrical family. His father, Carl Friedrich (1770-1813), was not only a police actuary but also a keen amateur actor. Albert (1799-1874), Richard's elder brother, became a high tenor and later a stage manager. The five daughters, Rosalie, Luise, Klara, Maria Theresia and Ottilie, were named after heroines in Goethe and Schiller.

Carl Friedrich, the father, died very shortly after Richard's birth, and his mother Johanna married the actor, dramatist and portrait painter Ludwig Geyer (1779-1821). It was Geyer whom Richard had to thank for his earliest theatrical experiences. The family soon moved to Dresden where Geyer had been hired as a character actor. He smuggled his young stepson into rehearsals, and soon Richard was himself on stage in various comedies. He recalls figuring in one of these as 'an angel, entirely sewn up in tights and with wings on my back, in a graceful, though laboriously studied, pose'.[4] It was actually as a cupid; but Wagnerian autobiography, however entertaining, has always to be read with caution.

Richard was especially close to his actress eldest sister, Rosalie (1803-37). Her career blossomed, and when the Royal Saxon Court Theatre in Leipzig reopened on 2 August 1829 it was she who was chosen to speak a specially written Prologue.[5] This was followed by a performance of Shakespeare's *Julius Caesar*, given in August Wilhelm Schlegel's translation.

Most theatres then alternated performances of plays, operas and ballets. Shakespeare's works were the nucleus of the repertory. This was not surprising. For Shakespeare had

---

in the programme book for the production of the *Ring* at the Royal Opera House, London, 1991; Daniel H. Foster, *Wagner's 'Ring' Cycle and the Greeks* (Cambridge: Cambridge University Press, 2010).

3. A notable exception is Yvonne Nilges' dissertation *Richard Wagners Shakespeare* (Würzburg: Königshausen & Neumann, 2007).

4. *My Life* (*Mein Leben*), trans. Andrew Grey, ed. Mary Whittall (Cambridge: Cambridge University Press, 1983), p. 5. Subsequently *ML*.

5. By Theodor Hell.

long since been hugely influential in Germany. Goethe and many others virtually regarded him as a German: had not Hamlet been educated at Wittenberg?[6]

The plays given in Leipzig included not only *Julius Caesar* but also *King Lear*, *The Merchant of Venice*, *Much Ado About Nothing*, *Othello*, *Hamlet* and *Macbeth*.[7] Rosalie was the company's young romantic lead, her roles including Cordelia, Portia, Beatrice, Desdemona and Ophelia. And of course her teenage brother, long since enthused by the Bard, saw all of these.[8] He was already a fervent disciple, and in 1826 had thrown himself heart and soul into the English language, producing 'a metrical rendering of Romeo's monologue into German as its first-fruit'.[9]

Young Richard's Shakespearean education also owed much to his uncle Adolf (1774-1835), his father's younger brother, of whom he speaks with gratitude and affection in *Mein Leben*. As a young man Adolf had known Schiller and he became a literary scholar and linguist of no mean accomplishment, with an international perspective that was exceptional for the time. He translated copiously from Greek, Latin, Italian and English with equal facility, his publications including editions of Burns, Byron and translations of Augustine Skottowe's *Life of Shakespeare* (1824) and of Mrs [Anna Brownell] Jameson's *Shakespeare's Heroines* (1832).[10]

Disliking the travesties to suit fashionable taste that were the rule in most Shakespearean performances that the young Richard would have seen, Adolf was the enthusiastic director of, and participant in, readings of the plays in the homes of his friends. In his nephew, Adolf could not have found a more eager pupil. Young Richard had been boarded out in Leipzig with him for some weeks in the summer of 1822. But it was when his family moved there from Dresden at the end of 1827 that Richard was able to spend long and profitable hours with his mentor. In *Mein Leben* Wagner recalled how:

> Every day I picked him up for his afternoon constitutional around the gates of the city. I imagine that we frequently provoked the amusement of passers-by, who overheard our profound and frequently heated discussions.[11]

---

6. See, for example, Roger Paulin, *The Critical Reception of Shakespeare in Germany 1682-1914* (Hildesheim: Georg Olms, 2003). I am most grateful to Professor Paulin for his kind advice and for a copy of Julius Petersen's 1930 article on Ludwig Tieck's Berlin production of *A Midsummer Night's Dream* of 1843 (which is fully referenced in note 25).

7. Translations by August Wilhelm Schlegel, except for *Macbeth*, where the translation is by Schiller.

8. Although Wagner saw a great many Shakespeare plays in his youth, it is not until 1844 that we have a reasonably documented account of what he would actually have seen.

9. William Ashton Ellis, *Life of Richard Wagner*, vol. 1 (London: Kegan Paul, Trench, Trübner and Co. Ltd, 1900), p. 93.

10. The titles of Adolf's translations are: *William Shakespeares Leben* (Leipzig: 1825) and *Frauenbilder oder Charakteristik der vorzüglichen Frauen in Shakespeares Dramen* (Leipzig: 1834). The original title of Mrs Jameson's book was *Characteristics of Women: Moral, Poetical, and Historical*. It was subsequently changed to *Shakespeare's Heroines: Characteristics of Women: Moral, Poetical, and Historical*. It is regarded as a seminal feminist study, and has often been reprinted.

11. *ML*, p. 23.

Illustration 2: The 15-year-old Wagner on his afternoon tutorial walk with Uncle Adolf, as depicted in watercolour in 1880 by Isolde, his 15-year-daughter. On the right, a scene from *Leubald*, a sin of the composer's youth, presided over by its inspiration, Shakespeare.

Those discussions would doubtless have engaged with the fastidious Adolf's appalled censure of his pupil's *Leubald*, a five-act tragedy:

> to which Shakespeare, principally through *Hamlet*, *Macbeth* and *Lear*, and Goethe, through *Götz von Berlichingen*, had contributed. … nothing I had gathered from tales of chivalry, nor anything I had garnered from *Lear* and *Macbeth*, was left out. … One of the main ingredients of my poetic fancy, I owed to Shakespeare's mighty language, emotional and humorous. The boldness of my grandiloquent and bombastic expressions particularly upset and amazed my uncle Adolf.[12]

There could be no more eloquent testimony to the importance of Adolf and Shakespeare in Richard's young life than the picture by his daughter Isolde.

It comes from an album of year-by-year watercolours – a sort of 'Daddy, this is your Life' – presented to her father on his sixty-seventh birthday in 1880.[13] Isolde was then 15, exactly the same age as her father when he wrote *Leubald*. Of all the 1828 events

---

12. *ML*, pp. 25-27. The complete German text of *Leubald: Ein Trauerspiel* was published for the first time in the 1988 *Bayreuther Programmheft* for *Die Meistersinger*, together with an article in German, English and French by Isolde Vetter describing the complex provenance of a text which for many years was considered lost.

13. Dagny R. Beidler, *Für Richard Wagner! Die 'Rosenstöcke-Bilder' seiner Tochter Isolde* (Cologne/Weimar/Vienna: Böhlau, 2013).

Illustration 3: Isolde Wagner's depiction of Ada conjuring Arindal back to life in Act Three of *Die Feen* (The Fairies) by singing to his lyre.

she could have chosen, it is surely significant that she depicted, on the left, her father taking his regular afternoon walk at the Leipzig city gate with Adolf, his mentor in 'everything serious and exalted in the realm of knowledge',[14] and on the right a scene from *Leubald*. The hero, appropriately in a blood-red cloak, strikes a Hamlet-like pose among a handful of the eight corpses he'd slain (the total body count is eighteen). A portrait of Shakespeare hovers above.

The author believed that his 'work could only be judged rightly when provided with the *music* I had now decided to write for it'.[15] That was not to happen. But he pressed ahead with his musical studies. Thanks to the recommendation of his elder brother, the singer Albert, Richard, now 20, became chorus master in Würzburg in 1833. Choral duties were not his only ones, for he had to take speaking parts in plays and even swell mime groups in the ballet.

Die Feen **and** Das Liebesverbot

At the same time, he began his first opera, *Die Feen* (The Fairies). Though he modelled it on Gozzi's story 'La donna serpente', Wagner unsurprisingly imports Shakespearean elements, including a mad scene in Act Two for its hero, Arindal, that is plainly borrowed from *King Lear*. In Gozzi, Arindal's wife, Ada, is transformed into a snake. But Wagner is surely remembering *The Winter's Tale* when he has Ada not transformed into a snake but petrified into a statue. And Ada is miraculously restored to life through the power

---

14. *ML*, p. 23.
15. *ML*, p. 27.

Illustration 4: Wilhelmine Schröder-Devrient, 'daughter of the great Shakespeare', as a trouser-role
Romeo in the tomb-scene of Bellini's *I Capuleti e i Montecchi*, known to Wagner in
its German version, *Romeo und Juli*a.

of music (Arindal singing to a lyre) just as Hermione is in *The Winter's Tale* in response
to Paulina's cry, 'Music: awake her: strike!'[16]

Unfortunately, Wagner was unable to secure a performance of *Die Feen*. It was never
given in his lifetime – its premiere had to wait until 1888 under Franz Richter in Munich.
I was lucky enough to have caught the first performance after the Second World War.
This was given by the Bayreuth Youth Festival in 1967, with my future wife Jill Gomez
in the role of Lore, sister to Arindal.

The following year, 1834, Wagner moved to Magdeburg as full music director. Within a
few months he was swept off his feet by the great singing actress Wilhelmine Schröder-
Devrient.[17] She was playing Romeo (a travesty role) in Bellini's *Romeo und Julia*, the
German-language equivalent of *I Capuleti e i Montecchi*; this is actually based not on
Shakespeare but on an Italian novella (1554) by Matteo Bandello.[18] We could perhaps

---

16. Plainly there is a common precedent in Ovid's story of the sculptor Pygmalion, whose
    infatuation with the beauty of the statue he has made charms it into life. But Wagner's
    debt is most obviously to Hermione in *The Winter's Tale*.
17. It was actually back in Leipzig in March 1834.
18. Bandello's novella was known to Shakespeare through his immediate source in Arthur
    Brooke's narrative poem *The Tragicall Historye of Romeus and Juliet* (1562). But there are
    considerable differences between Shakespeare's version of the story and that of Bellini's
    librettist, Felice Romani.

think of her as the Maria Callas of her day, though she would have paid less attention to the notes on the page.

A few years later in Paris, in November 1839, Wagner was bowled over by Berlioz's great Shakespearean interpretation of *Romeo and Juliet* in his dramatic symphony. Wagner could have paid no greater compliment to Berlioz than with the palpable echoes of the symphony's adagio love-theme that resound through *Tristan und Isolde*.[19]

In Schröder-Devrient Wagner discovered the soprano of his dreams – a singer who was as powerful an actress as she was a singer. Heinrich Laube, a close friend of Wagner's, described her as 'the daughter of the great Shakespeare, a descendant of the Greek gods'.[20]

Within a few months, in June 1834, and fired up by this experience, Wagner turned to Shakespeare's *Measure for Measure*, or *Mass für Mass*,[21] as his model for a new opera, *Das Liebesverbot* (The Ban on Love). It had to be subtitled 'The Novice of Palermo' in order to placate the censor, and was a shameless bid to capture the high ground of Italianate opera that he was later so vehemently to deride.

Wagner would certainly have had Schröder-Devrient in mind for his Isabella in *Liebesverbot*. The opera is an exceedingly free adaptation of *Measure for Measure*, Wagner calling in Shakespeare to support the libertarian programme of the radical Young German movement to which he himself belonged:

> All I cared about was to uncover the sinfulness of hypocrisy and the artificiality of the judicial attitude toward morality. Thus, I departed from *Measure for Measure* entirely and let the hypocrite be punished only by the avenging power of love.[22]

The finales of both acts of *Liebesverbot* end in un-Shakespearean populist uprisings. And Wagner crudely rewrites the ambivalent and darkly troubling ending of the play, with Isabella launching a call to arms:

Ihr Heil'gen, welche Schändlichkeit! …	*(Holy saints, what villainy! …*
Greift zu den Waffen! Auf zur Rache!	*Seize your weapons! Vengeance!*
Stürzt ihn, den schändlichsten	*Topple this most shameful tyranny!)*
Tyrannen!	

---

19. In an 1857 essay on Liszt's symphonic poems, Wagner praises Berlioz's *Roméo et Juliette* but ticks him off for following Shakespeare's play too faithfully, arguing that as a dramatic *composer* he should have allowed purely musical considerations to have determined the shape of his symphony. The message is that composers, once inspired by a literary drama, should transform it into a superior, because quintessentially *musical*, drama. Wagner surely acknowledged his debt in the inscription in the score of *Tristan und Isolde* he presented to Berlioz: 'To the dear and great composer of "Romeo and Juliet", the grateful composer of "Tristan and Isolde".' In Berlioz, the Shakespearean influence was of course far more direct and pervasive than in Wagner.

20. Oswald Georg Bauer, *Richard Wagner Goes to the Theatre*, trans. Stewart Spencer (Bayreuth: Bayreuth Festival, 1996), p. 35.

21. As he knew it in Christoph Martin Wieland's translation.

22. *ML*, p. 83. Wagner's detailed description of the action is in *ML*, pp. 113-18.

Illustration 5: To the left of Isolde's spreading tree, the finale of *Das Liebesverbot* (The Ban on Love) in which Isabella and the King are married, a flagrant departure from Wagner's source in *Measure for Measure*. On the right of the tree, Schröder-Devrient's Romeo has his shapely leg well over the parapet in the balcony scene from Bellini's *I Capuleti e i Montecchi*.

Could there be an embryonic *Götterdämmerung* Brünnhilde here too?

In Isolde's picture for 1834, the wicked German killjoy Friedrich (Shakespeare's Angelo), is seen to the left, repentant, with his wife Mariana. And we can see that, because Isolde is thinking of Shakespeare's Duke, she has Isabella marry the King. The scene on the right takes us back to Bellini's *Romeo und Julia* with Schröder-Devrient as Romeo, and an unknown Juliet.

The first performance of *Das Liebesverbot*, conducted by Wagner after ten days' rehearsal, was famously a fiasco. The advertised second performance was abandoned after backstage fighting broke out between Isabella's real-life husband and her real-life lover, the young and handsome tenor playing Claudio. The handsome tenor retreated to his dressing room with a bloodied face. So much, we may think, for the opera's celebration of free love.

In 1837 Wagner moved to Riga as music director. It was there, he tells us, that he enjoyed 'extremely good performances' of *Hamlet*, *The Merchant of Venice* and *King Lear*.[23] The indelible impression that *Lear* left on him is testified by Isolde's inclusion of the play as a key experience of 1838.

To the left is a scene from Méhul's *Joseph en Égypte* (Joseph in Egypt, in the German version known to Wagner *Joseph in Ägypten*) which Wagner much admired and conducted in Riga, while the central image is of the concluding conflagration in *Rienzi* on which he was working at the time. In Bulwer Lytton's novel, the composer's primary source, it is Rienzi's *wife* who heroically perishes with him in the Capitol. But in

---

23. Bauer, *Richard Wagner*, p. 46.

Illustration 6: Isolde's choice of significant experiences from her father's time in Riga: Méhul's *Joseph en Egypte* (Joseph in Egypt), the Capitol on fire at the end of *Rienzi*, Wagner's work-in-progress, and King Lear raging in the storm.

Wagner's version it is Rienzi's *sister* Irene, surely a reincarnation of Isabella in *Measure for Measure*.

Ludwig Tieck's 'authentic' *Midsummer Night's Dream*

In January 1844 Wagner travelled to Berlin to conduct the first performance there of *Der fliegende Holländer* (The Flying Dutchman). In the very same theatre, the Schauspielhaus, the other sensational theatrical event of the season was also playing. It had begun life in the much smaller theatre in the royal palace at Potsdam. This was *A Midsummer Night's Dream*, staged by Ludwig Tieck (1773-1853), an important pioneer of the romantic movement and a good friend of Wagner's uncle Adolf.

Tieck had been a passionate Shakespearean since his student days in Göttingen.[24] In London, in 1817, he had met Coleridge and seen John and Charles Kemble and Edmund Kean in *Julius Caesar*, *Macbeth*, *Richard II* and other plays.[25] He had also studied Edmond Malone's researches (from 1790) into Shakespeare's Globe and the Rose and Fortune theatres, including the original builder's contract for the square-plan Fortune

---

24. 1793-94.
25. Largely, Tieck thought, 'disappointing performances' of *Cymbeline* (with John Kemble), *Julius Caesar* (both Kembles), *Henry VIII* (John Kemble), *Macbeth* (Kean) and *Richard II* (Kean). Roger Paulin, *Ludwig Tieck: A Literary Biography* (Oxford: Clarendon Press, 1985), p. 207 ff.

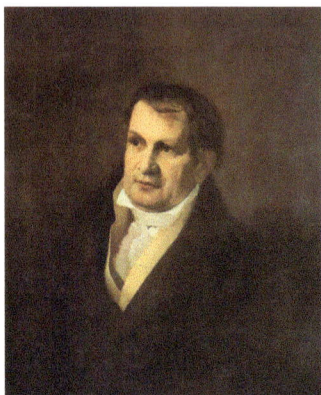

Illustration 7: Ludwig Tieck,
pioneer of the 'authentic'
performance of classic
drama. Portrait by Robert
Schneider, c.1833.

Illustration 8: Felix Mendelssohn,
whose well-known incidental music
was commissioned for Tieck's
sensational 1843 staging of *A
Midsummer Night's Dream*. Portrait
by Theodor Hildebrandt, 1835.

which Malone had found among Philip Henslowe's papers.[26] Tieck was well known as novelist, poet and critic, but his lifelong ambition was to put on *authentic* performances of the Greek and Elizabethan classics. This had foundered on the conservatism of most theatre managers and their defence of freedom to make the habitual wholescale adaptations. In 1840 Tieck was eking out a rather miserable life in Dresden. And then, at the age of 69 he was suddenly summoned to Berlin by Friedrich Wilhelm IV, who had just come to the Prussian throne. He was given a generous pension and a free hand to put on Greek plays and those by Shakespeare in whatever way he liked in the king's private theatre in the royal palace.[27]

He had long dreamt of staging Shakespeare not, as was the invariable practice, behind a proscenium arch in an Italianate theatre, but on an open stage, with minimal scenery and props, and surrounded by the audience. He wanted the words, the acting, to do the talking, not beautiful scenery.[28] We are back with the 'Muse of Fire' prologue to *Henry V*:

---

26. Andrew Gurr, 'Shakespeare's Globe' in J.R. Mulryne and Margaret Shewring (eds.), *Shakespeare's Globe Rebuilt* (Cambridge: Cambridge University Press, 1997), p. 27.

27. Court order of 22 June 1842. Julius Petersen, 'Ludwig Tiecks Sommernachtstraum-Inszenierung', *Neues Archiv für Theatergeschichte* 1 (Berlin 1930), p. 166.

28. While dramaturg at the Dresden Court Theatre (1825-42), Tieck had already taken a step towards the Shakespearean theatre. In 1836 he had collaborated with Wagner's republican friend the great architect Gottfried Semper on the construction of a theatre modelled on his knowledge of the historic Fortune, but which rejected that theatre's thrust stage in favour of 'a broad, shallow relief stage' and 'two conspicuous flights of stairs [which] led to a substantial upper stage.' Simon Williams, *Shakespeare on the German Stage, vol 1: 1586-1914* (Cambridge: Cambridge University Press, 1990), p. 178, and illustration, p. 177.

let us, ciphers to this great account,
On your imaginary forces work. ...
Think, when we talk of horses, that you see them
Printing their proud hoofs i' th' receiving earth:
For 'tis your thoughts that now must deck our kings,
Carry them here and there: jumping o'er times;
Turning th' accomplishment of many years
Into an hour-glass.

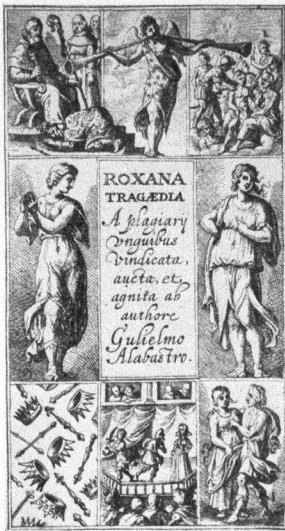

Illustration 9: Tieck's slender information about the reality of Shakespeare's theatres came from the small panel (middle of the bottom row of images) on the title page of Gugielmo Alabastro's tragedy, *Roxana*, published in 1632. It shows a performance in the Red Bull theatre in Clerkenwell some time after 1605.

Wagner had reason enough to attend Tieck's *Midsummer Night's Dream*, not least because Tieck's story, 'Der getreue Eckart und der Tannenhäuser' (Faithful Eckart and Tannenhäuser, 1799) was a source for *Tannhäuser*, the very opera on which he was currently working. And there would have been his covert curiosity about the incidental music for *A Midsummer Night's Dream*, specially commissioned from a rival, Felix Mendelssohn, the court's music director. (The well-known overture had been written much earlier, in 1826.)

Illustration 10: Notice the spectators in the stage boxes and the curtains flapping behind the performers in this detail of the Red Bull stage from the *Roxana* title page.

With hindsight we know that despite his assiduous research, Tieck's understanding of the Elizabethan stage was far from perfect. The only visual image he had was a vignette, supposedly of the Red Bull theatre in Clerkenwell, which opened around 1605. The vignette was part of the title page of a Latin-verse play *Roxana* (*c.* 1595) by William Alabaster that wasn't printed until 1632.

Tieck knew that a Shakespearean theatre would have had an apron stage, pillars supporting an upper storey, a retiring house in the middle and a balcony.[29] But how could he hope to create any of this in the king's baroque private theatre at Potsdam?[30]

---

29. Petersen, 'Ludwig Tiecks Sommernachtstraum-Inszenierung', pp. 175-76.
30. Built in 1763-69.

Illustration 11: The first performances of Tieck's
Midsummer Night's Dream took place at Potsdam in
the Royal Theatre of the Neues Palais. Built in 1769,
it is a jewel of a Baroque theatre, this photo showing
the front of the auditorum and
part of the proscenium.

Illustration 12: The amphitheatre of the Royal Theatre. It is hard to imagine how it
could have accomodated Mendelssohn's orchestra of fifty for *A Midsummer Night's
Dream* as well as the privileged courtly audience.

The theatre was so small that Tieck couldn't even hope to extend the stage forward through the proscenium arch. He therefore concentrated on using the space *behind* the proscenium to come, as closely as he could, to the Shakespearean stage as he understood it. He commissioned designs from Johann Karl Jacob Gerst, the Court's principal scenic artist (and, incidentally, also the designer for the *fliegende Holländer* performances).[31] Gerst created three different levels for performance, dividing the stage into nine 'boxes'. The boxes could be curtained off with rug hangings, thus permitting the action to proceed continuously, while 'settings' for the next scene were created behind the rugs.[32] The design for Act Three (Shakespeare's Act Five, the wedding of Theseus and Hippolyta) clearly shows the nine 'boxes' and the steps.

There is little question that Tieck's vision must have been seriously compromised by the superfluity of performers, without which the king and the audience would doubtless have considered themselves short-changed.[33] The small theatre had

Illustrations 13 and 14: From J. K. J. Gerst's 1843 designs for *Ein Sommernachtstraum*.
Above, Titania's bower. This, was created in the central 'box' on the lower level, as shown below in the setting for the wedding scene. The pillars framed the entrance to Theseus's palace, from which he and Hippolyta made their entrance. The fairies, tumbling all over the steps, created what Fanny Mendelssohn called 'a moment of pure magic'.

---

31. Gerst's 'designs' for the Berlin *Der fliegende Holländer* were little more than instructions to borrow bits of scenery from productions of the Royal Opera House's repertory operas. As that theatre and its scenic store burnt down on 18 August 1843, we have no idea of what was eventually improvised, its performances being necessarily transferred to the smaller Schauspielhaus. See: Patrick Carnegy, *Wagner and the Art of the Theatre* (New Haven and London: Yale University Press, 2006), p. 31.

32. Much use of the steps was made for entrances and processions, though one curmudgeonly reviewer complained that Theseus and Hippolyta's wedding procession, accompanied by Mendelssohn's famous March, managed to do little more than process up a flight of stairs, turn around and then come down again to the same place. Petersen, 'Ludwig Tiecks Sommernachtstraum-Inszenierung', p. 187.

33. One is reminded of Richard Strauss' *Ariadne auf Naxos* in which the Major-Domo reproaches the Composer for not coming up with anything more fitting for his master's

Illustration 15: So successful was the Tieck/Mendelssohn *Midsummer Night's Dream* that it moved
to a far larger theatre, Karl Friedrich Schinkel's Schauspielhaus on the Gendarmenplatz
in Berlin. Coloured engraving, c.1821, of the newly opened theatre.

to accommodate Mendelssohn's orchestra of some 50 players, and there were more than
100 performers on stage. Eyewitnesses, including Mendelssohn's sister Fanny, extolled
the way in which Tieck had the fairies – children from the ballet school – tumbling
down the steps and everywhere bewitching the stage. Whatever the shortcomings,
the novelties of the production made it a huge hit[34] and it soon transferred to the very
much larger Schauspielhaus on the Gendarmenmarkt, where Wagner was to see it.

Here's how Titania's bower scene looked in the Schauspielhaus (Illustration 16).

Tieck's production cannot have failed to impact upon the 30-year-old Wagner. And
it came at a critical stage in his career. His responses[35] were muted by envy of the far
greater success of *A Midsummer Night's Dream* – his own *fliegende Holländer* in the
same theatre being withdrawn after a mere four performances – and most particularly
by envy of Mendelssohn's music. But it seems to me more than likely that Tieck's hugely
successful *Midsummer Night's Dream* may have nudged Wagner away from the heroic,

---

luxuriously appointed theatre than a scene set on a desert island.

34. Seven performances had to be given in the first ten days, and in all the piece was given 40
    times: Bauer, *Richard Wagner* (see note 20), p. 88. Up to 1885, when it was eventually
    abandoned, there were 169 revivals (Williams, *Shakespeare on the German Stage,* note 28,
    p. 185). Tieck's production laid the foundations for performances in Germany right
    through the nineteenth century, and echoes of it resound right through to Max Reinhardt's
    film version of 1935, starring James Cagney as Bottom, Mickey Rooney as Puck and Olivia
    de Haviland as Hermia, with massed fairies choreographed by Bronislava Nijinska.

35. In *Oper und Drama*, 1850, and later in *Mein Leben*.

legendary matter of *Der fliegende Holländer, Tannhäuser* and *Lohengrin*, and towards the richly rounded, human world that, quite exceptionally for him, he was to dramatize in *Die Meistersinger*.

For it was in 1845, only a year after the Berlin *Midsummer Night's Dream*, that Wagner first sketched his idea for what was intended to be a compact, comic opera, a 'jovial Satyr-play'[36] that would be easy to perform and would make him a lot of money.[37] Although the principal textual sources for *Die Meistersinger* are the accounts by Gervinus and Wagenseil of the Nuremberg Meistersinger guilds of the sixteenth century, there was surely no little encouragement in that direction in Shakespeare's confident handling of his down-to-earth mechanicals, quite possibly seen by Wagner as caricature, parodistic versions of the cobblers, bakers and tailors he was to portray in *Die Meistersinger*. Professor Roger Paulin, Tieck's biographer, nicely suggests that 'one might perhaps see Wagner's Hans Sachs as a kind of

Illustration 16: There was very much more room for the orchestra and players of Tieck's *Midsummer Night's Dream* in the Schauspielhaus. Abundant foliage, partially concealing the steps, framed Titania's bower in the lower, central 'box'. Wagner's *Der fliegende Holländer* also performed in the Schauspielhaus, and with scenery by Gerst, failed to enjoy the same success. The artist's impression is from the Leipzig *Illustrirte Zeitung*.

fulfilment of the Tieckian image of Shakespeare the actor-producer-poet'.[38]

Isolde Wagner's souvenir picture for 1845 shows first, to the left, the first performance of *Tannhäuser*, and then her father holidaying in Marienbad where he wrote the first prose sketch for *Die Meistersinger*. To the right we therefore see Hans Sachs with his shoes and Beckmesser with his lute.

If there is midsummer mayhem and madness in *Midsummer Night's Dream*, what else do we find in *Die Meistersinger*, the climax of which of course takes place on Johannistag, or Midsummer Day? It is surely not insignificant that Wagner knew Shakespeare's play through Christoph Martin Wieland's German translation, which was originally subtitled 'Ein St Johannis Nachts-Traum' – 'a St John's Night Dream'. And surely we can think of Beckmesser as a reincarnation of Malvolio from *Twelfth Night*, his yellow cross-gartered wooing of Olivia incredulously seen by her as 'very

36. *Ein heiteres Satyrspiel*, in 'Eine Mitteilung an meine Freunde' (1851), *Sämtliche Schriften und Dichtungen* (Leipzig: Breitkopf und Härtel, n.d.) vol. 4, p. 284.

37. *ML*, p. 303.

38. Paulin, *Ludwig Tieck*, p. 428.

Illustration 17: On 13 April 1845 Wagner finished *Tannhäuser*, its Wartburg location depicted on
the left in Isolde's watercolour. He and his then wife Minna recuperated with a five-week holiday
in Marienbad (middle picture) where on 16 July he completed his first prose sketch for
Die Meistersinger, and on 3 August a similiar text for *Lohengrin*. On the right we see
Isolde's idea of Nuremberg, with Sachs and Beckmesser in the foreground.

midsummer madness'.[39] Just like Malvolio, Beckmesser is 'notoriously abused'. Like
Malvolio, he finds his nemesis in discovering, and crassly misinterpreting, the writing
on a sheet of paper.

In Cosima Wagner's 1888 Bayreuth revival of *Die Meistersinger* she rescued
Beckmesser from being little more than the usual caricature by having him played by
Fritz Friedrichs, who was primarily known as an *actor* rather than a singer. Maybe not
cross-gartered, but the type is unmistakable. In David McVicar's 2011 Glyndebourne
production, Johannes Martin Kränzle gave a brilliantly Malvolio-esque performance
of the role.

Shakespearean echoes

Following the failure of the 1849 revolution in Dresden – in which Wagner took an active
part – the composer had a price on his head and had to flee Saxony for Switzerland.
His work was seriously held up, a contributory factor being the problem of how to find
the right form for the *Ring*. Although looking over his shoulder to Greek tragedy, he
saw that 'a single, closed drama' as espoused by the Greeks couldn't be of use to him.
So, now living in exile in Zürich, he put composition aside and embarked on a massive
exploration of theatrical and operatic history in order to map out his own way.

---

39. *Twelfth Night*, Act Two, iv, 55.

The resultant spate of writings includes the very substantial *Oper und Drama* in which he wrestled with Greek tragedy, with Shakespeare, Goethe and Schiller, as well as with his bête noire, the French neo-classical drama of Racine and Corneille. His reading of Shakespeare confirmed his intuition, that music-drama should fight free from the closed forms of French neo-classical theatre, and of operatic forms such as those of *opera seria* and *opéra comique*.

From Shakespeare he also seized on the integration of comedy into tragedy (we have to look no further than Mime's antics with Siegfried in *Siegfried* Act One, and the badinage between Alberich and Mime in Act Two), and learnt the tremendous dramatic advantage of being able to move rapidly from one scene to another without great pauses while complex scenery is changed behind closed curtains.[40]

Nevertheless, we do have to accept that, moulded from Greek and ancient Nordic and Germanic sources, the *Ring* inhabits a different dramatic world to Shakespeare's.[41] Its high ambition is to forge a myth-based drama rather than one of recognizably human behaviour. Yet, despite his mythopoeic bent, Wagner could not but help create characters and scenes, human and all-too-human, in which Shakespeare was surely his model and inspiration.

Illustration 18: 'I'll be revenged on the whole pack of you!' A Beckmesser with Malvolian ancestry: the actor Fritz Friedrichs in Cosima Wagner's 1888 production of *Die Meistersinger*.

Can we discern palpable Shakespearean echoes in the *Ring*? Here we have to be very careful in that many scenes reminiscent of Shakespeare have an ancestry stretching far back into theatrical history. But I think we *can* pin down an influence in the way Wagner twists material taken from his mythic sources. Take, for example, the Norns who open *Götterdämmerung*. In the Nordic Eddas they are simply described as setting the laws that seal men's fate. But Wagner has them actually *foretell* the future, just as he knew the witches do in *Macbeth* (and they, like

---

40. For the *Ring*, now in gestation, the possibility of moving between scenes on an open stage would be just the thing. Think only of *Das Rheingold* with its transitions between the bed of the Rhine, a high mountain landscape and Nibelheim within the bowels of the earth.

41. Yet … : 'In the imagination of the nineteenth century the Greek tragedians and Shakespeare stand side by side, their affinity transcending all the immense contrarieties of historical circumstance, religious belief, and poetic form.' George Steiner, *The Death of Tragedy* (London: Faber, 1961), p. 192.

the Norns, set the scene for the entire work).[42] A further influence from *Macbeth* is detectable in the characterization of Ortrud in *Lohengrin*. In the medieval sources, notably poems by Wolfram von Eschenbach, Ortrud merely seeks to inflame the *people* against Lohengrin and Elsa. But in Wagner's Ortrud we have a veritable Lady Macbeth poisonously working on her husband to usurp power. 'Ortrud', the composer told Liszt on 30 January 1852, 'is a woman who *does not know love* … Her nature is politics.' Indeed, *Macbeth*, which he read in Schiller's translation (1801), was always one of his favourite plays. In May 1878 Cosima records his comments after rereading Act One: 'The whole daemonic nature of life is set before one's eyes, naked, beyond all deception.'[43] One cannot help but wonder whether, five years earlier, he might not have been momentarily tempted when, as Cosima records on 17 December 1873, 'A man in Brussels asks "the giant philosopher" to compose a *Macbeth* and a *King Lear*.' Lady Macbeth is no less a felt presence in *Die Walküre*, as when Fricka cruelly urges upon Wotan the necessity of Siegmund's death, a notion not found in Wagner's sources.

In *Götterdämmerung*, where the 'real' world of Gunther and his court entangles with the mythic world of Wotan and the 'gods', the Shakespearean temper often takes over from that of Aeschylean tragedy. The Iago-esque scheming of the jealous Hagen and the wonderful scene of Alberich's ghostly exhortation of his slumbering son, 'Schläfst du, Hagen mein Sohn?', is a comparable scenario to that of the Ghost of Hamlet's Father urging him on to revenge. Even the rhythm of the Ghost's whispered parting words 'Adieu! Adieu! Hamlet, remember me' (in Wagner's German translation, 'Ade! Ade! Ade! Gedenke mein!') seems to be echoed in Alberich's 'Sei treu! Sei treu! Treu!'.[44]

In the closing scenes of *Götterdämmerung*, as Michael Ewans has well observed, we are far closer to Elizabethan and Jacobean tragedy, to 'the final scenes of *Hamlet* than to any surviving Greek tragedy': 'vengeance is met with counter-vengeance, Gunther fights Hagen and is killed, the hand of Siegfried's corpse rises up to repel Hagen's grab

---

42. The root of the name of Shakespeare's 'weird' sisters is 'Wyrd', itself derived from the OE 'Urd' meaning future or *fate*. The Eddas have the Norns drawing water at the Well of Urd and what do they weave but the rope of fate?

43. *Cosima Wagner's Diaries*, ed. Martin Gregor-Dellin and Dietrich Mack, trans. Geoffrey Skelton, vol. 2 (London: Collins, 1978), p. 78 (27 May 1878). From an earlier reading of the play: 'In the evening *Macbeth*, the impact of which is again a crushing one. "As with Antony, Hamlet, Othello, Shakespeare shows us in Macbeth a character entirely destroyed by Fate. Of the Macbeth as he is described to us and honoured in the beginning there is no trace left, the demonic takes control, and the individual ceases entirely to exist. That is the play's greatness and tragedy."' *Cosima Wagner's Diaries*, vol. 1 (London: Collins, 1978), p. 241 (3 July 1870).

44. Consider also Lennox's description of the eerie atmosphere before Macduff's discovery of Duncan's murder: 'The night has been unruly … / Lamentings heard i' th' air, strange screams of death … the obscure bird / Clamoured the livelong night . ….' Does this not foreshadow Gutrune's foreboding of Siegfried's death: 'Nein! Noch kehrt er nicht heim. Schlimme Träume störten mir den Schlaf!' (No! He still hasn't come home. Nightmares have disturbed my sleep!)?

Illustration 19: The antithesis of the Shakespearean theatre: Wagner's 'Greek' amphitheatre in the Bayreuth Festspielhaus. Photograph c. 1930 with, on the stage, the hallowed 1882 scenery for the Temple of the Grail.

for the ring.'[45] Even if 'born in myth', Wagner's characters tend to act as though well-schooled in the humanity, infinite variety and unpredictability of Shakespeare's.

The Festspielhaus and the 'Gesamtschauspieler'

By 1870 the *Ring* was substantially complete. In a new spate of writings, beginning with the marvellous centennial essay on Beethoven,[46] Wagner looks back to Shakespeare the actor-playwright and the self-evident truth that actors on an open Elizabethan stage had no other option than to inhabit their characters and deliver them to the groundlings with maximum intensity. Wagner himself was a formidable improvisational actor, in real life as well as when directing his performers.

He was keen there should be a permanent record of his rehearsals for the 1876 premiere of the complete *Ring*, and entrusted the task to his assistant Heinrich Porges. Porges' invaluable account shows just how closely Wagner felt he was leaning on Shakespearean practice, even if his Festspielhaus, with its proscenium stage, could not have been further from the exposed, apron stage of the Elizabethans. It was in fact the ultimate peep-show theatre, the stage framed by a double proscenium arch to heighten the sensory illusion.

Blithely turning a blind eye to this, Porges writes:

---

45. Michael Ewans, *Wagner and Aeschylus* (London: Faber, 1982), pp. 205-06. The quotation is adapted.
46. A new translation and introduction by Roger Allen (Woodbridge: Boydell Press, 2014).

Illustration 20: Cosima records how, at home in Wahnfried in his later years, 'R' read aloud, and doubtless enacted, Shakespeare on a great many evenings. In Wilhelm Beckmann's oil painting, probably from 1882, R is holding forth to Cosima, her husband Liszt, and the composer's disciple Hans von Wolzogen.

Illustration 21: For Wagner's grandson Wieland, the point of departure for his radically brilliant productions was the Shakespearean empty stage.

The principles governing [Wagner's] style of dramatic presentation were essentially in accord with Shakespeare's. As if by magic, [Wagner] could assume at a stroke any role in any situation – indeed … he demonstrated these powers so fully it was as though he himself were the 'total actor' (*Gesamtschauspieler*) of the entire drama.[47]

Wagner's acting skills were scarcely less on display than when at home in Wahnfried. A picture from 1882 shows Cosima on the left, with her father holding forth both to Liszt and to his fervent disciple Hans von Wolzogen on the right. It appears that Wagner read Shakespeare aloud almost every evening. This was an immersion in the plays for the sheer joy of it, an enlivening passion of the composer's later years. It is pre-eminently a sense of awestruck admiration that tumbles from Cosima's diary. She describes how they read through the plays again and again. The only ones she doesn't mention are *The Comedy of Errors*, *Troilus and Cressida* and *The Two Noble Kinsmen*. Sometimes she gives just a few lines recording how impressed they were by this or that passage. But there are longer accounts that show just how discerning Wagner could be, as, for example, when he asserts that to make its full effect, *Richard III* should not be performed on its own but always as the sequel to the *Henry VI* trilogy.[48]

Once the first festival was over, Wagner had on his mind not just substantial revisions for

---

47. Heinrich Porges, *Wagner Rehearsing the 'Ring'*, trans. Robert L. Jacobs (Cambridge: Cambridge University Press, 1983), p. 3.
48. *Cosima Wagner's Diaries*, vol. 1, p. 47 (24 January 1869).

Illustration 22: Midsummer magic 'without Nuremberg': Hans
Hotter as Sachs in the second act of Wieland Wagner's
1956 *Meistersinger*.

the staging of the *Ring*, but also what would be the scarcely less problematic staging of *Parsifal*. It began to dawn on him, but sadly too late, that the solution lay in renouncing every-leaf-on-every-tree representation in favour of playing to the theatre of the spectator's imagination, just as he had long since applauded Shakespeare for doing. It was in that idea, that concept of theatre, that the most fruitful ways of realizing Wagner upon the stage took root.

After Wagner's death in 1883, his widow Cosima notoriously put the clock back in a futile attempt to perfect the imperfectible peep-show theatre of illusion. But in the long run (as I show elsewhere) it was the Shakespearean perceptions of the Swiss theatre-artist Adolphe Appia that were to triumph, most especially in the post-war Bayreuth of the composer's grandsons Wieland and Wolfgang Wagner. For the most part Wieland cleared the stage of scenery, using little more than lighting and abstract forms in his designs, and severely restrained the acting.

The point was to ask the spectators to allow the sheerly musical drama to act on their imaginations and emotions.

The Shakespearean stage: Wieland Wagner and Joachim Herz

There could have been no more appropriate belated tribute to Wagner's Shakespearean inspiration than Wieland's 1956 and 1963 stagings of *Die Meistersinger*, the composer's opera most palpably indebted to Shakespeare and *A Midsummer Night's Dream*. Wieland's 1956 production faced up to the Shakespearean ghost hovering in the background. In the second act he cleared the stage so completely of anything representational – and, so shortly after Hitler's war, there were obvious political reasons for so doing – that the staging became known as 'Die Meistersinger ohne Nürnberg'. Wieland had wanted to rescue the opera from having become what he called 'a dangerous mixture of Lortzing and the Reichsparteitag'.[1] And so he rejected specific invocation of sixteenth-century Nuremberg in favour of a bare minimum of visual reference.[2]

In the second act we are in Shakespeare's world with the intrigues of a midsummer night taking place on an open promontory, above which floats a floriferous sphere. Wieland said he had intended 'the romantic irony of a Shakespearean midsummer night'.[3] This was the first time the picturesque half-timbered scenery had been totally removed, and of course it created a furore in Germany. In London *The Times* took a more dispassionate view:

> Wieland Wagner's production of *Die Meistersinger* has set musical Germany by the ears. ... The setting [of Act Two], though impractical at times, has an arresting beauty of its own, and it allows Wagner's midsummer eve magic to work its potent spell on the mind of the listener, and evoke the Nuremberg which the designer has avoided.[4]

For Wieland's biographer, Walter Erich Schäfer, it was the 'solution of the century'.[5]

Four years later, in the then very different political and cultural ambience of East Germany, Shakespearean echoes were more palpably invoked in Joachim Herz's 1960 production in Leipzig. Herz's inspiration was to frame the action of *Meistersinger* within a galleried Elizabethan theatre. The basic elements were wooden galleries ranged down either side of the stage. In Act One they were used to suggest the nave of a church of late medieval ambience.

1. Interview in *Hessische Nachrichtung*, 27 July 1956, cited in Geoffrey Skelton, *Wieland Wagner: The Positive Sceptic* (London: Gollancz, 1971), p. 134.
2. For the third-act *Festwiese* Wieland took us back to the Greeks, playing the 'action' on a circular 'orchestra', with behind it the chorus immobilized and commenting from an amphitheatre that seemed to mirror the paying audience in their own amphitheatre.
3. Cited in Frederic Spotts, *Bayreuth: A History of the Wagner Festival* (New Haven and London: Yale University Press, 1994), p. 219.
4. Cited in *Ibid*, pp. 219-20.
5. Cited in *Ibid*, p. 219. For the political rationale behind the production, see 'Reinventing Wagner after Hitler', Chapter 6 in this book.

Illustration 23: The East German director Joachim Herz, who sought to lay the ghosts of Nazi appropriation by reimagining a Shakespearean theatre on his Leipzig stage.

For the third-act festival meadow, the galleries were finally revealed as part of an open-air theatre, with a raised trestle-stage standing in the centre ready for the song contest. Illustration 24 shows Walther launching into his Prize Song.

Wieland Wagner came to see Herz's production, was impressed, and shamelessly stole the idea of a Globe-style setting as the starting point for his second Bayreuth production in 1963. He, too, staged significant scenes as though within a Renaissance theatre. In the finale, the principal singers shared the same space with an 'audience' in the shape of the chorus. This staging, like Herz's, was of course limited in

Illustration 24: Joachim Herz, with his designer Rudolf Heinrich, staged the finale of *Die Meistersinger* as though in an open-air courtyard theatre characteristic of the early Jacobean period. On the trestle-stage Walther (Gustav Papp) is performing his Prize Song, with the Masters seated in the foreground.

its Shakespearean ambition by the nineteenth-century proscenium theatre in which it was performed. Both directors sought to compensate by building the Globe's auditorium galleries into the stage setting.

In the concluding scene of Act Three, Anja Silja's Eva is seated centre-right with Jess Thomas' Walther, in black, standing slightly below her and to the left. The scene in the festival meadow had begun with the rough-and-tumble of a Bruegel-like interpretation of the Apprentices' Dance that evolved into a conga, with the girls from Fürth drawing the entire company into a single human chain. Fanfares from trumpeters on papier-mâché horses heralded the arrival of the guilds, with banners not of their trades but of the Nine Muses (which Beckmesser in Act Two had desperately called to his aid!). 'The whole impression', wrote Wieland's biographer Walter Panofsky, 'was that of an improvised farce like the play of Pyramus and Thisbe presented [in Shakespeare's play] by Peter Quince to the court.'[6] But then the atmosphere turned more serious for the arrival of the Masters, the 'Wach' auf' chorus in praise of Sachs, and the song contest itself.

The effect of both Herz's and Wieland's productions was to exorcize the malign spirits of the past and to show that *Die Meistersinger* was much more than an anthem to German nationalism. The invocation of Shakespeare, Wagner's perennial passion, had surely been in every way appropriate, and, indeed, redemptive.

Illustration 25: A Globe-style theatre is more closely referenced by Wieland Wagner, in Act Three of his 1963 production, than by Herz. Eva (Anja Silja) sits on a carnival float surrounded by banners of the Nine Muses, with Walther (Jess Thomas) standing just below her.

---

6. Walter Panofsky, *Wieland Wagner* (Bremen: Schünemann, 1964), p. 76.

Illustration 1: Alfred Pringsheim in 1875,
the year before he recorded his impression
of the final rehearsals for the Bayreuth premiere of the *Ring*.

Chapter Two

Reckoning up the *Ring*[1]

A Mathematician's Diary of Bayreuth 1876

It is always exciting when a previously unknown account of the *Ring*'s parturition at Bayreuth in 1876 comes to light. And particularly so when the witness turns out to be Alfred Pringsheim (1850-1941), father-in-law of that great Wagnerian, Thomas Mann. Although Pringsheim's day job was as a professor of mathematics, a field in which he achieved considerable distinction, he was a pianist of near-professional standard. Around 1863 he was swept away by a performance of *Tannhäuser* and Wagner became a lifelong passion. The eighteen manuscript pages of the diary recording his attendance at rehearsals in the Festspielhaus from 5 to 21 July 1876 contain no major surprises but are of great interest none the less. For the 25-year-old Pringsheim tempers his passion for the composer and his music with a clear-sighted critical perspective. So many of our

1. Source: *The Wagner Journal*, vol. 8, no. 2, July 2014, pp. 52-58. My warm thanks to Tash Siddiqui and Jim Ford for their help in teasing Pringsheim's parody into English.

Wo sich Aug' und Ohren laben,
Will die Nase auch was haben.

Illustration 2: Raising a glass in anger: a cartoon of the 'Schoppenhauer' incident when Pringsheim assaulted an unimpressed fellow witness of the *Ring*'s premiere with his well-loaded beer-mug. The doggerel caption might be freely translated: 'When eyes and ears refreshment seek / A jar of ale will smash the beak'.

most important sources for the 1876 *Ring* are those of Wagner's starry-eyed musical assistants like Heinrich Porges and Julius Hey: yet the more dispassionate accounts, among which Richard Fricke's *Bayreuth vor dreissig Jahren* (1906) stands supreme, and to which Pringsheim's must now be added, are of especial value.

Born in 1850, the year of *Lohengrin*'s Weimar premiere under Liszt, Pringsheim came from a seriously wealthy family. His father, Rudolf, had made his money from the railways, and the Pringsheims lived in style on a small estate. Alfred studied mathematics at Heidelberg and while still a 21-year-old student became one of the first subscribers to the *Patronatschein* scheme launched to fund Bayreuth. Pringsheim bought no fewer than three *Patronatscheine* – quite an outlay (approximately equivalent to €20,000 in modern terms) – and it's likely that he, and very possibly other members of his family, gave further financial support. Cosima's *Diary* suggests that the Wagners continued to have expectations from the Pringsheim direction. The next year (1872) Pringsheim went to Bayreuth for the laying of the foundation stone for the Festspielhaus and probably met Wagner. Thereafter he vigorously took up the cudgels in print against many of the composer's crasser critics. In 1873 he published *Richard Wagner und sein neuester Freund – eine Erwiderung auf Herrn Dr Gotthelf Häblers 'Freundesworte'* (Richard Wagner and his Most Recent Friend – A Retort to Dr Gotthelf Häbler's 'Words from a Friend'), followed in 1874 by *Glossen zur Wagner-Kritik* (A Commentary on Criticisms of Wagner). These and sundry other writings are included in *Alfred Pringsheim, der kritische Wagnerianer: Eine Dokumentation*, edited and introduced by Egon Voss, chief editor of the complete edition of Wagner's works, and with contributions by Dirk Heisserer, chairman of the Thomas Mann Forum in Munich and editor of the series in which the book appears.[2]

Pringsheim became the scourge of ill-informed and prejudiced criticism, particularly that directed against the composer's easily mocked libretti. The words, he insists, only find their poetic meaning when combined with the music for which they were intended. Wagner's epochal achievement was the *Gesamtkunstwerk* in which the words and the

---

2. Egon Voss (ed.), *Alfred Pringsheim, der kritische Wagnerianer: Eine Dokumentation* (Würzburg: Königshausen & Neumann, 2013).

music were inseparable. Pringsheim champions Wagner against all comers. In Nietzsche's *Richard Wagner in Bayreuth* (hot off the press when Pringsheim discussed it in his diary entry of 14 July 1876) he finds 'much beautiful and true, but even more half-true and blind – overall it's nonsense'.

Illustration 3: The music room in the Arcisstraße neo-Renaissance villa occupied by Alfred Pringsheim and his family from 1890.

During the first festival itself – which Pringsheim believed would resolve all doubts about the *Ring* as consummate *Gesamtkunstwerk* – and after the premiere of *Siegfried* on 16 August 1876, the passionate young Wagnerian got into an argument in Angermann's famous bar with a Shakespearean scholar, Professor Leo, to whose derogation of the composer he responded by thwacking him on the nose with his beer-mug, thus earning him the sobriquet of 'Schoppenhauer' (beer-mug belligerent: any echo of the synonymous philosopher would be ironic – Pringsheim the positivist mathematician was not at all of his pessimistic persuasion). The precise nature of the altercation and its repercussions are expertly unravelled in Voss' book. Later, there was also a duel with pistols (no blood was drawn on either side), Pringsheim's adversary this time being the Berlin theatre critic Dr Isidor Kastan.

What is clear is that 1876 confirmed Pringsheim's lifelong avocation as a Wagnerian, not only prepared to punish antagonism with a well-aimed beer-mug, but also gifted with a sense of humour rare among the faithful. In 1877 he presented his future brother-in-law, the Berlin banker Hermann Rosenberg, with a rare copy of the first public printing of the *Ring* text (1863) in which he inscribed an affectionate parody of the verse. The dedication is on the blank page following the page with the title, which is the understood subject of what follows:

[Der Ring des Nibelungen]	[The Ring of the Nibelung]
Den Wagner wirkte 　aus Weh und Wonne, 　aus Weltenwahn 　und Weltenweisheit, 　der Worte Wurzeln 　weise verwebend zum Wunderwerke; den mit „Bappe" band 　der Binder der Bücher 　in lichten Leders leuchtende Hülle; des nordischen Nibelungs 　rächenden Ring, 　in des Rheines Fluthen 　Vom Fluche gereinigt, reich' ich, o Rosenberg, Dir: auf daß Du ihn lesest, 　wenn die Lust Dich lockt, 　und Du deßen gedenkest 　der Dich lieben ihn lehrte.	Which Wagner worsted 　from woe and well-being, 　from wanton world 　and world's own wisdom, 　the web of words 　wisely woven into wonderworks; which were basted and bound 　by the binder of books 　in lustrous leather's luminous shell; the Nordic Nibelung's 　ring of revenge, 　by the Rhine's coursing current 　cleansed of its curse, I render to you, dear Rosenberg: reasoning you may read it, 　when leisure allows, 　and remember the one 　who led you to love it.

For a *Fasching* party at his house in 1894, Pringsheim concocted a wickedly irreverent scena, *Der Bajazzo* (The Clown). Billing himself as 'Diebitsch Motivinski' (Thieving Motivinski), he stole the title from the usual German one for Leoncavallo's *Pagliacci* which had been premiered two years before. Its text (reproduced in full by Voss) and music subjected snippets from Wagner's operas, interwoven with others from *Cav* and *Pag* (*Cavalleria rusticana* and *Pagliacci*), *Hänsel und Gretel*, *Aïda* and *The Mikado*, to the indignity of *commedia dell'arte* parody with Motivinski himself directing and playing the title role.

In December 1876, Breitkopf published Pringsheim's two-piano version of the 'Schluß-Scene aus *Tristan und Isolde*', the first of the many Pringsheim arrangements that were to follow and which receive excellent discussion in Voss' book. The latter also includes biographical and critical material by Voss and Heisserer who valuably fill out the picture that has painted Pringsheim principally as a wealthy mathematician and father of Thomas Mann's wife, Katia. The artistic patronage he exercised in his palatial Munich house at Arcisstrasse 12 – where he amassed a famous collection of Renaissance majolica – is already familiar from many accounts, not least the descriptions of musical evenings in Mann's *Diaries*, Monika Mann's *Erinnerungen*, and in Erika Mann's eightieth-birthday tribute to her grandfather. Pringsheim's music room included two concert grands, and Voss suggests that he would very probably have played with such regular visitors as Hermann Levi, Richard Strauss, Bruno Walter and their like.

Pringsheim's diary pages were discovered in the Franz Wilhelm Beidler-Archiv in Winterthur, Switzerland (Franz Beidler was the husband of Isolde, Wagner's first child by Cosima, and Franz Wilhelm Beidler was their son). Extracts were published by Dagny Beidler (Franz's granddaughter) and Eva Rieger in the *Frankfurter Allgemeine*

Zeitung on 22 February 2013, but Voss' *Alfred Pringsheim* is now the first publication of the complete Bayreuth diary – or rather as much of it as has survived.

It begins on 5 July 1876 with Pringsheim settling himself into the Reichsadler Hotel and at 5 p.m. plunging in by attending a full rehearsal (scenery and costumes) of the Prologue and first act of *Götterdämmerung*: 'Großartiger Total-Eindruck, doch im Einzelen noch vieles zu wünschen übrig' (Tremendous impression of the whole, but details leave much to be desired), thus encapsulating Pringsheim's characteristic response in which enthusiasm is tempered with critical observation. After *Götterdämmerung*, the rehearsal schedule begins again with *Rheingold*, Pringsheim hearing everything through to the end of *Siegfried* Act Two on 21 July, when the diary breaks off.

Pringsheim likes the simplicity of the Festspielhaus auditorium and the novelty of the curtain not rising but parting in the middle. On entering, 'the theatre is so dark that you cannot see your hand'. He finds that eventually you get used to it but still have to struggle to read – confirming that the gas lamps were turned low and not actually extinguished. Although making no comment on the novelty of the hidden orchestra pit, Pringsheim is very concerned about the inaudibility of many passages familiar to him from the scores, and about the balance. In the first act of *Götterdämmerung*, 'in many places the wind and brass completely kill the strings', though he goes on to suggest that the emptiness of the auditorium could be partly to blame. At the piano-only rehearsal of the second act the next day, he reports that in the soft passages you could hardly hear anything (he surely means of the piano), but that in the loud ones everything became unclear: 'It was as though every musical, poetic and dramatic accent was obliterated in a dreadful fortissimo.' Pringsheim tactfully avoids attributing this to his friend Joseph Rubinstein's exertions at the piano, which was presumably placed in the pit.

At the following day's rehearsal of the same act with full orchestra, Pringsheim finds that the piano run-through hadn't given any idea of its magnificence. His high point is Hagen's Summoning of the Vassals; but he finds the ensuing Vengeance Trio, which reminds him of Ortrud and Telramund in the second act of *Lohengrin*, 'the most difficult and hard to understand part of the whole work'. After further study at the piano in his room, Pringsheim decides that with the exception of the scene with the vassals, this act is musically below the level of the work as a whole: 'Alongside its many beauties one finds great stretches of absolutely boring music, a whirlpool of motifs, a bizarre jumping between the most distant intervals, then again nothing less than the melodic motif in the bass (Hagen's revenge) rushed into inaudibility, the vocal lines unbelievably mistreated.' Much of this he is prepared to blame not on Wagner – and he avoids any mention of Richter's conducting – but on the 'miserable acoustics': 'you couldn't hear a single fine detail in the orchestra, the rich violin figurations almost totally lost, and for long stretches you couldn't catch a single syllable of the text.' He doubts whether even a full audience would help, but Rubinstein tells him that everything Wagner intended would then come across perfectly.

Be that as it may, Pringsheim's impressions of the singers (many of whom he came to know while drinking with them late into the night at Angermann's) are often illuminating. While finding Karl Hill admirable as Alberich in the second act of *Götterdämmerung*, he thinks his voice lacks in sonority and that you can hardly understand any of his text. Franz von Reichenberg, standing in as Hagen, has

Illustration 4: Pringsheim's description of Valhalla as looking 'like a synagogue, an Indian tomb or a collection of antique standard clocks' chimes with this oil painting by the *Ring*'s original designer, Josef Hoffmann, for the closing scene of *Das Rheingold*. Hoffmann's contribution to the *Ring* is discussed in the Chapter 3, which includes the artist's oil sketch for the same scene.

a reasonable voice but is 'dramatically and musically no better than a herd of cattle'. When he meets Gustav Siehr, the actual Hagen, he wraps him up as an 'Opernsänger … without any real understanding of Wagner's art'. This was evidently no obstacle to Pringsheim furthering the acquaintance, Siehr later telling him that Wagner – as is of course now common knowledge – was always glad to allow singers a measure of freedom. Albert Niemann (Siegmund), whom Pringsheim considered the epitome of a truly dramatic singer, later tells him that although Wagner himself wanted a fast tempo for the wonderful E major section in the final act of *Tristan* ('Wie sie selig, / hehr und milde / wandelt durch / des Meers Gefilde?'), he and the conductor Karl Eckert, performing the work in Berlin in March 1876 (when it was rehearsed by the composer himself), had taken it very much slower.

Pringsheim finds Georg Unger's Siegfried 'better than I'd imagined', the young Siegfried in that work suiting him better than the one in *Götterdämmerung*. In *Rheingold* he praises Heinrich Vogl's brilliant Loge (his music contrasting with the 'dry-recitative style' of Wotan's). Friederike Sadler-Grün's Fricka 'totally lacks dramatic impression', Froh (Unger) sings 'dreadfully', while the giants (Albert Eilers and Franz von Reichenberg) are too insignificant and fail to dominate their scenes. In the first act of *Walküre*, Niemann is great as Siegmund, but although Josephine Schefsky sings well

enough as Sieglinde, she 'has no idea about acting and fluid movement'. Pringsheim
has high praise, *passim*, for Franz Betz's Wotan and Wanderer, but finds the narration
in Act Two of *Walküre* 'too long'.

His remarks always demonstrate his awareness that much inevitably goes wrong
in rehearsal and his hope that apparent deficiencies will be ironed out, or at the least
pale into insignificance, when the work as a whole is performed. On 12 July he plays
through the third act of *Götterdämmerung* at the piano, finding it even more 'colossal'
than he'd previously thought. At the rehearsal later that day he finds it:

> indescribable. The three Rhinedaughters sing fabulously. – Siegfried's murder,
> the Funeral March and final scene probably achieving the highest tragic
> impression of anything known to me. Seeing that now without costumes, with
> only half the scenery, the stage machinery incomplete and with continual
> stoppages and disturbances, this creates so powerful an effect, what must be
> the effect created by a proper, completed performance? ... On the way home
> I ran into Wagner. He was very friendly, complaining he'd presently so little
> time for his friends as at the moment he could only be a machine.[3]

The following day there is no rehearsal and Pringsheim is among the guests at a
Wahnfried party where the high-spirited Wagner tells stories and, when Karl Hill
(Alberich) declines, himself sings ballads by Loewe accompanied at the piano by
Karl Eckert. Pringsheim's reportage of Wagner's discourse captures his idiosyncratic
verbosity: 'Ne, ne, ne – der Halévy das ist ein naiver Mensch gewesen [...]. Ah, die *Jüdin*
schätze ich sehr hoch; ne, ne, ne sagen Sie mir nichts gegen die *Jüdin*; ah, der 2te Act ist
ja ganz coloßal'. (No, no, no – Halévy that was a naive fellow [...]. Ah, I greatly value
La Juive; no, no, no, don't say anything to me against *La Juive*; ah, the second act is
quite extraordinary.)

A day or so later (19 July) Pringsheim is excited to receive his copy of the newly
published full score of *Götterdämmerung*. After a thunderously applauded rehearsal of
the third act of *Die Walküre*, he is with Levi, Betz, Niemann and Hill at Wagner's table in
the theatre restaurant. The composer exuberantly holds forth, prompting Pringsheim
to echo Niemann's opinion that it is 'an insoluble riddle how this little man with his
Saxon conviviality can have written all these great works'.

Pringsheim's primary interest is in the music, but he does offer a few observations
on the scenery and stage direction. He finds the settings for the Valkyrie Rock and
Gibichung Hall, with its view to the Rhine, very beautiful. In the stage direction
of Hagen and the vassals, 'Wagner the *régisseur* shows himself in all his glory'.
In *Rheingold* he rates the bed of the Rhine 'very beautiful' but in Scene 2 (the open
space on a mountain summit) is impressed by 'neither the flowery foreground, nor
the castle of Valhalla in the background which looked like a synagogue, an Indian
tomb or a collection of antique standard clocks'. This is close to the critic Wilhelm
Mohr's description of 'a whole series of towers of various heights which looked like
massive carriage-clocks or gravestones'. The transitions to and from Nibelheim are 'of

---

3. Voss, *Alfred Pringsheim*, p. 151.

Illustration 5: The eighty-year-old Alfred Pringsheim (centre) with his wife Hedwig at his son-in-law's
Baltic-coast summer house at Nidden in 1930. To the right is Thomas Mann, and to the left
Mann's son Golo (holding his sister Elisabeth) and his daughter Monika.

great beauty'. No mention of the 'steam curtain' that was used, but this could have been because the boilers hadn't yet been fired up. Not a word about the rainbow bridge.

In *Die Walküre* Pringsheim thinks the Act One decorations not as good as they had been at King Ludwig's royal-command performance in Munich (premiere 26 June 1870), and that:

> the Valkyrie scene is presently spoiled by the defective optical projections [from magic lantern slides] of the galloping Valkyries ... and the extraordinarily difficult musical ensemble of the eight Valkyries is not yet faultless. But I'm sure the effect of this scene will be magnificent.[4]

The Magic Fire he considers to be a great improvement on Munich. When it came to *Siegfried*, he couldn't come to any view of the 'Drachenscene' in Act Two because the monster itself hadn't yet arrived from London: 'Fafner's singing through the loudspeaker is a uniquely grotesque effect.' And with those words the diary comes to an end.

Pringsheim must surely have continued his account, but no further pages from it appear to have survived. Fate has played a strange trick in breaking off the diary at almost the same place that the composer laid the *Ring* to one side. We can only guess whether Pringsheim thought Wagner's magnificently re-energized resumption of the *Ring* with the third act of *Siegfried* made up for his feeling that in the second act much was amiss. He liked Siegfried's solo scenes, found the scene with the Wood Bird 'wonderfully poetic' but otherwise thought that much of the act was 'zu viel Unmusik'

---

4. *Ibid*, p. 156.

[too much non-music] – an agglomeration and juxtaposition of material, lacking any organic flow.

Pringsheim returned to Bayreuth for the first complete *Ring* performance, 13-17 August, but unfortunately there is no record of what he made of it. Two years later he married Hedwig Dohm (1855-1942) and they were both present at the *Parsifal* premiere in 1882, returning again to the Festspiele in 1888, 1891, 1908 and 1930. In 1933 Pringsheim courageously defended Mann against the infamous 'Protest der Richard-Wagner-Stadt München', whipped up against Mann's brilliant lecture 'The Sorrows and Grandeur of Richard Wagner' for its daring to set the composer's genius in a clear-sighted critical light. (The signatories to the Protest shamefully included Hans Knappertsbusch, Hans Pfitzner and Richard Strauss.)

Pringsheim was swiftly denounced as 'not of Aryan stock' and a few months later Arcisstrasse 12 was compulsorily purchased for the Nazi Workers' Union (NS-Deutschen-Arbeiterverein). It was the beginning of the end. In 1939 he and his wife escaped to Zürich where they settled in close proximity to the Manns. As an 85-year-old, Pringsheim accompanied his grandson Michael Mann (subsequently a professional violinist) in Mendelssohn's Violin Concerto. His love of Wagner remained right through to his death in 1941. Only the year before, he had celebrated his ninetieth birthday by playing the piano part in his piano quintet arrangement of the *Siegfried Idyll*.

Illustration 1: Wagner commissioned the Viennese landscape painter Josef Hoffmann as designer for the first complete performance of the *Ring* at Bayreuth in 1876. This portrait photo dates from c. 1890.

Chapter Three

Designs on the *Ring*[1]

The mystery surrounding Josef Hoffmann's original sketches unravelled

Despite the voluminous documentation, we still have to struggle for a clear picture of what the *Ring* actually looked like at its Bayreuth premiere in 1876. There are posed studio portraits of the singers in their costumes, but no photographs of the actual scenery and production. The best visual evidence, until comparatively recently, was a set of fourteen monochrome photographs of the Viennese artist Josef Hoffmann's stage designs. These had been taken by Victor Angerer at the artist's request and published in a handsome portfolio as a memento. One of these sets was obtained by Wagner's patron, King Ludwig II, and hung by him in the writing room of his hunting lodge on the Schachen. The original designs had disappeared without trace. We could only guess how Hoffmann's painterly interpretations of Wagner's detailed instructions would have looked in colour.

---

1. Source: 'Designs on the *Ring*', *The Wagner Journal*, vol. 4, no. 2 (July 2010), pp. 41-55.

This was the case until the early 1990s, when some large *Ring* paintings by Hoffmann miraculously came to light in a castle on the Rhine. Then in 2005 the artist's preliminary oil sketches for Wagner (fourteen in all) were discovered by Max Oppel, a Munich dealer. It was Oswald Georg Bauer, sometime dramaturg of the Bayreuth Festival, friend of Wolfgang and Gudrun Wagner, and leading authority on Wagnerian iconography, who first identified the paintings in the castle and set in motion the protracted negotiations which led to their acquisition by the Richard Wagner Museum at Haus Wahnfried and the inaugural exhibition there in 2006. They were published in the Festival Programme Book in 2006 and then in *Die Szene als Modell*, the book accompanying the Wahnfried exhibition, which also illustrated seven of the oil sketches. These paintings and all the oil sketches are now beautifully reproduced in Dr Bauer's enthralling book, *Josef Hoffmann: Der Bühnenbildner der ersten Bayreuther Festspiele* (Josef Hoffmann: The Stage Designer of the First Bayreuth Festival).[2] But, as I shall explain later, Bauer has not quite told the complete story.

Rightly excited by his discoveries, Bauer has researched the shadowy figure of Hoffmann, who had disappeared from history almost as completely as his designs for the most momentous operatic event of the nineteenth century. The Hoffmann to whom we're now introduced is no hack painter of scenery but, like Wagner himself, a firebrand theatrical revolutionary, not to mention a very considerable painter by any standards. The composer knew exactly what he was doing in choosing him for Bayreuth. That the two of them fell out so disastrously, just as Wagner was finishing the score of *Götterdämmerung*, is a reflection of the similarity of their uncompromising personalities.

Early career

Hoffmann was born in Vienna on 22 July 1831. As a 17-year-old he entered the venerable Academy of Fine Arts as a student of 'classical and life drawing'. But this was 1848 and the revolutionary upheavals of that year compelled him to abandon his course after no more than three months. Thereafter he broke out on his own, travelling widely through Europe, drawing and painting everywhere he went. Returning to Vienna, he studied (1851-52) with Carl Heinrich Rahl. One of the leading names in Austrian landscape painting, Rahl had rebelled against the political clampdown at the Academy after 1848 and set up an independent school of his own. His aim was to rescue historical painting from what he saw as a rising tide of scientific discoveries that threatened to destroy allegory, undermine fantasy and reduce the artist to no more than a functionary.

The young Hoffmann was deeply sympathetic to all this. Rahl encouraged an appetite for travel which was to take Hoffmann through the Balkans, to the Salzkammergut, Innsbruck, and thence to Venice where he spent the winter of 1856. The following year he was off sketching ruins in Greece before settling for six years in Rome, where he enjoyed the friendship of Peter Cornelius, Friedrich Overbeck, Friedrich Preller the Elder and other artists of the German colony there. One of the finest fruits of his early work as a painter of idealized classical landscapes is the *Ancient Greek Landscape with Bacchantes and the Grave of Anakreon*, completed in 1865, which now hangs in the

---

2. Deutscher Kunstverlag: Munich and Berlin, 2008.

Academy of Fine Arts. Reminiscent of the style of Claude Lorrain, its roseate homage to the classical world anticipates his later visualizations for the *Ring*.

Hoffmann's first foray into designing theatre sets came in 1869, when he was called in to help the Vienna State Opera's resident scenic artist, Hermann Burkhardt, with Gounod's *Roméo et Juliette* and Auber's *La Muette de Portici*. None of these designs appears to have survived, but Hoffmann's contribution must have been valued, for he was quickly given sole responsibility for designing a new *Zauberflöte*. The word 'sole' is important for two reasons, first because he disliked working with anyone else (as they with him), and secondly because he sought total coordination between settings, props and costumes. (The general practice was for landscape and architectural scenes to be assigned to separate artists, while costumes were yet another speciality.) Of course Wagner himself also sought a unified overall effect, but was not averse to employing diverse talents to achieve it.

Hoffmann interested himself in all aspects of stage design and technology (as a ground plan for *Der Freischütz* and his three surviving models for the *Ring* testify). Like most other scenic artists of his time, his aim was the creation of settings as historically correct as they could be. For *Die Zauberflöte* this meant the presentation of an ancient Egypt that had been academically researched and not just fancifully imagined. The result (despite Hanslick's dismissal of it as 'an exhibition of Egyptian art' surpassing even *Aïda* in its superficial extravagance) was acclaimed in Vienna as a pinnacle of historical representation, winning Hoffmann a new commission for *Der Freischütz* in 1870. Archaeology may not have been so helpful here, but the streak of nightmare romanticism (*Schauerromantik*) in Hoffmann, coupled with his technical know-how, helped him conjure up a Wolf's Glen so terrifying that all Vienna wanted to see it.

Designs for the *Ring*

Meanwhile, Wagner had been casting about fruitlessly for someone to design the Bayreuth *Ring*. He was determined to find a 'real' artist and not just a decorator of stages. Names he very likely considered include a 'Herr Wernicke [*sic*] in Dessau' (doubtless the F. Wernecke who had designed the Gluck *Orfeo ed Eurydice* that Wagner had seen in December 1872 in Dessau), the Austrian artist Hans Makart and the Swiss painter Arnold Böcklin, later famous for *The Isle of the Dead*. He made an approach to the landscape specialist Heinrich Döll (who had worked on all of King Ludwig's Munich stagings of Wagner's operas) but this was declined. Bauer shows that it was not, as is often thought, Carl Brandt who eventually drew his attention to Hoffmann but a young Viennese medallist, Anton Scharff, for whom Wagner, then living at the Hotel Fantaisie, was sitting for a relief medal shortly after the laying of the foundation stone for the Festspielhaus in May 1872. Over the summer Wagner and Hoffmann corresponded, with the result that the composer commissioned from him a set of preliminary sketches that led to the artist being contracted to design the *Ring*.

Although evidently impressed by Hoffmann's mountain landscapes, Wagner and Cosima found his architectural treatment of interiors like those of Hunding's hut and the Gibichung Hall far too 'historical'. They asked for changes, which Hoffmann was evidently unwilling to effect. For the Wagners it was important that, in keeping

Illustration 2: Photograph by Victor Angerer of Josef Hoffmann's small-format oil sketch for the closing scene of *Das Rheingold*.

Illustration 3: Hoffmann's oil sketch for the same scene. The artist's large oil painting of the same scene is reproduced in the preceding chapter, 'Reckoning up the *Ring*'.

Illustration 4: Hoffmann's large oil painting of Siegfried's arrival at the Hall of the Gibichungs
in the second act of *Götterdämmerung.*

with the mythopoeic ambition of the *Ring*, the settings should not fix the work in any
historical time or place, so here already was a fundamental difference with a painter
famed for being able to do just that (or, rather, to convince audiences of the authenticity
of his depictions). In the end it was not Wagner's rigidity but Hoffmann's that was, so to
speak, the unfortunate rock on which the partnership foundered. Hoffmann necessarily
had to work with Carl Brandt and the Coburg scenic studio of Max and Gotthold
Brückner if his designs were to be translated into stage reality. But he was irked by
having to deal with these formidable theatrical practitioners. Wagner did his best to
mediate but came to dread meetings at Wahnfried, when Hoffmann invariably proved
inflexible.

So, as is well known, Wagner dropped the disgruntled Hoffmann, entrusting the
realization of his designs (with the modifications that the artist had resisted) to the
Brückners and Brandt. Hoffmann and his wife did return for the premieres in 1876 when,
perhaps mischievously on someone's part, they were quartered in the same lodgings
(Reuerweg 699) as the Brückners. We can only guess at the artist's reaction to what
he would surely have considered the misrepresentation of the world *he* had imagined
for the *Ring*. This impression would have been reinforced because the Festspielhaus'
illumination (gas and partial electric lighting) of the painted scenery would have been
markedly inferior to what Hoffmann had been used to at the Vienna Opera. Although
he had been properly paid off, the artist remained entitled to the copyright in his designs
and understandably sought to exploit this through, inter alia, the sale of Angerer's

photographs of them. It is at this point that the plot begins to thicken.

During the 1876 festival there was an exhibition in the Neues Schloss of paintings, photographs and other objects connected with Wagner's works. The exhibits included the Angerer photographs, together with 'Josef Hoffmanns prächtige Farbenskizzen zu den scenischen Entwürfen zum *Nibelungen Ring*' (Josef Hoffmann's magnificent colour sketches for the scenery of the *Ring of the Nibelung*) and costume sketches by both Hoffmann and Carl Doepler, the latter being the ones that were actually used for the first performances. With the discovery of the fourteen oil sketches (20.8 × 26 cm) in Munich we can see that these are indeed the very ones photographed by Angerer and that they are identical with the 'Farbenskizzen' of the exhibition listing.

Hoffmann's much larger paintings (literally 'Entwürfe', or draft designs; 82.5 × 107.5 cm) are an idealized documentation of what he thought the scenery should look like. In effect he was saying to Wagner, the Brückners and the world in general that this was what the

Illustration 5: Hoffmann at the height of his Wagnerian fame, depicted with palette and paintbrush as his shield and spear on the front of the Vienna satirical magazine *Der Floh* (The Flea), 18 March 1877.

Ring would, and indeed should, have looked like had he been allowed to complete his work. The paintings were plainly produced to be sold to help recoup his losses in the venture. It seems only right that they should have been bought by another supreme theatrical dreamer, Wagner's patron King Ludwig.

Since his first privileged sight of the oil sketches in April 1875 when Wagner had lent them to him, the king had remained enthusiastic about Hoffmann. Sometime after 5 September 1876 he acquired the worked-up paintings, quite possibly directly from Hoffmann himself. (To complicate matters still further, Bauer speculates that the indefatigable Hoffmann may at that time have painted more than one set of these eminently saleable pictures; more, as we shall see, were to follow later.)

Ludwig valued them highly not just as souvenirs of what he had (and had not!) seen on the Bayreuth stage, but as works of art in their own right. But a mere month or so after he had received the paintings, Hoffmann borrowed them back to be the centrepiece in yet another Wagner exhibition opening in Vienna on 7 December 1876. They were greatly admired as landscapes painted 'mit viel Schwung und Energie' (with considerable flair and energy), one critic observing that they would have been even better without the figures.

The king duly received his *Ring* paintings back, two years later commissioning from Hoffmann a set of seventeen watercolours to mark his royal-command performances

Illustration 6: Model of the interior of the Gibichung Hall from the Vienna Exhibition, 1892, with Hoffmann playing the part of an archaeologically correct early German. The wall paintings, however, are typical only of the decorative style that was to become characteristic of the Viennese Secession.

of the *Ring*, which took place in the Munich Court Opera in November 1878. Hoffmann had to swallow the pill that the scenic designs were not his but those of Ludwig's court painters Heinrich Döll, Christian Jank and Angelo II Quaglio. Doubtless it was to preserve his *amour propre* that he described the watercolours as 'self-sufficient works, unrelated to an actual stage representation'. These purely fanciful imaginings have disappeared, all that survives being photographs of eight of them which were taken by the king's photographer Joseph Albert and which are now in the museums of the Bayerische Verwaltung der Staatlichen Schlößer, Gärten und Seen. The first five (for *Das Rheingold* and *Die Walküre*) date from 1878, the remaining three (for *Götterdämmerung*) from 1885. After Ludwig's death in 1886, Hoffmann tried to retrieve his large oil paintings, but without success. By 1892 he had given them up as 'verschwunden' (missing). Bauer believes the original paintings were sold by the king's estate and quite possibly bought by the art collector and dealer Johann Georg Ehni, who subsequently sold them on to private customers.

* * *

Back in 1876, it is evident that Hoffmann's star was still very much in the ascendant on his home ground of Vienna, despite his rebuff by Bayreuth. On 6 December that year, the day before the Richard Wagner Exhibition opened there, the Court Opera secured from Wagner the right to the first performance outside Bayreuth after 1876 of *Die Walküre*. It was agreed that Hoffmann's designs would be used and that he himself would paint the scenery though, at his request, he was assisted by two of the theatre's resident artists, Gilbert Lehner and Alfred Moser. Hanslick was not alone in hailing the results (*Neue Freie Presse*, 7 March 1877) as more impressive than what had been achieved at Bayreuth, but no visual record of them appears to exist.

On the front of the satirical magazine *Der Floh* (The Flea), Hoffmann was fêted in a cartoon showing him as 'Ein Ritter von Pinsel und Palette', a Germanic Wotan with huge beard and winged helmet, wielding a paintbrush as his spear and a monster palette as his shield. (Illustration 5) But his triumph was to be short-lived. True to form, the intransigent artist fell out with his colleagues and the Court Opera went on to complete its *Ring* with other artists (Carlo Brioschi, Hermann Burghardt and Johann Kautsky).

Hoffmann successfully pursued his career in other directions that included more Greek landscapes and a fine set of murals for Vienna's Natural History Museum which exist to this day. There is also a superbly dramatic painting of the terrible fire that destroyed the Ringtheater on 8 December 1881 with the loss of some 400 lives. Appropriately enough, it is now to be seen in the city's Fire Brigade Museum.

This was not, however, the end of Hoffmann's Wagnerian involvement, for he was put in charge of the extensive Wagner section at Vienna's 1892 International Music and Theatre Exhibition. Having failed to recover any of his King Ludwig paintings, Hoffmann set about producing a set of copies for the exhibition and these found ready buyers. Unhampered by Wahnfried's anti-historical bias, the exhibition enabled him to indulge to the full his archaeological knowledge of the lives of the early Germans. He built a richly accoutred Gibichung Hall, with soaring pillars and encrusted with weaponry, then had himself photographed in it costumed as an ancient German.

On the walls, representations of the World Ash Tree anticipated the sinuous, decorative manner of Viennese *Jugendstil* and confirm the mix-and-match nature of *fin-de-siècle* 'historicism'. In a photo of the exterior of the Hall, Hoffmann reappears as Hagen brooding over the Rhine, and maybe over his so sadly troubled involvement with the *Meister*.

There were further world travels in 1893-94, an exhibition of paintings produced during them and continuing activities as a teacher, designer, art critic, lecturer and town planner. Hoffmann remained industrious right up to his death on 31 January 1904 at the age of 72, by which time he had completed hundreds of paintings and thousands of drawings. Only relatively few appear to have survived. Let us hope that more will be discovered both in public and in private collections, like the one from which the *Ring* paintings have recently emerged.

Discovery and acquisition by Bayreuth

I must now return to the story of how the Hoffmann paintings came to light. In 1990 a Bayreuth friend of Bauer's sought his advice after a relative in Worms had been shown some paintings which seemed to her just like images (the Angerer photos) reproduced in Bauer's book, *Richard Wagner: The Stage Designs and Productions from the Premieres to the Present*.[3] These paintings belonged to Baroness Barbro von Heyl zu Herrnsheim of the Schlößchen (Little Castle) next to the cathedral in Worms. Five small colour photos were sent to Bauer, who said to himself: 'If these are what I think, then this is sensational.' The Baroness was unfortunately not well, so it was not until February 1993 that he was able to visit her. She took him up to the attic and uncovered a large painting on an easel which Bauer immediately recognized as Hoffmann's vision of the finale of *Das Rheingold*. The other four were plainly part of the same series. Remembering that in the early thirteenth-century *Nibelungenlied*, one of Wagner's principal sources for the *Ring*, Worms was the location of King Gunther's castle, there could scarcely have been a more appropriate resting place for Hoffmann's pictures.

The following year the Baroness was invited to Bayreuth and sat with Wolfgang Wagner at a lecture in which Bauer for the first time showed slides of the discovered Hoffmanns (25 February 1994). There followed protracted negotiations which led eventually, ten years after their discovery, to the acquisition of the paintings by the Richard Wagner Museum, and their restoration and exhibition in 2006. This exhibition was also able to include the full set of fourteen oil sketches discovered by Max Oppel, which had similarly been bought for the Richard Wagner Museum. The provenance of the sketches remains unknown.

More was to come, for in February 2007 Bauer learnt that two further Hoffmanns (of an original set of three) had surfaced in the archive of the Gesellschaft der Musikfreunde in Vienna. These turned out to be impressionistic versions of the *Rheingold* finale and of the opening of the third act of *Siegfried*. They were identifiable from the catalogue of the 1892 Vienna Exhibition, their provenance is clear, and they are of especial interest in that they are landscapes without figures and in all probability were made for Wagner as a response to his criticism that the oil sketches had not done justice to his dramatic intentions. The third painting from this set has disappeared. Bauer believes that after the Anschluss in 1938 it may have been seized as a trophy by the Nazis because of its Germanic subject – it depicted the same exterior of the Gibichung Hall on the Rhine that Hoffmann had constructed for the 1892 exhibition and in which he had posed as Hagen. The two surviving paintings remain with the Musikverein in Vienna.

The five paintings from Worms had been in the possession of the Von Heyl family since their acquisition by Cornelius von Heyl, grandfather of Baroness Barbro's husband Siegfried, who had died in 1982. The likelihood is that Cornelius, a wealthy art collector and patron of the first Bayreuth Festival, acquired them sometime before 1 October 1888 from Georg Ehni, the art collector and dealer who had bought the greater part of King Ludwig's collection after his death in the Starnbergersee in 1886. Cornelius and his brother Maximilian had inherited the fortune that their father had made from his patent-leather factory. They were pre-eminent among German art collectors, Maximilian gifting his unrivalled collection of Böcklins to the Hessisches Landesmuseum in Darmstadt and his collection of Luther manuscripts to the

---

3. Trans. Stewart Spencer (New York: Rizzoli, 1983).

Illustration 7: Hoffmann's oil sketch of the end of the first act of *Die Walküre*.

Illustration 8: Hoffmann's later oil painting of the same scene as in Illustration 7. The double opening to the moonlit forest of the oil sketch has been replaced in this more softly toned version by a more dramatic single doorway behind Siegmund and Sieglinde.

Illustration 9: In Hoffmann's vision of a cavernous Nibelheim in *Das Rheingold*, Wotan and Loge are
capturing Alberich while at the far left Mime emerges from his hiding place behind a rock to exult.
There is no way this magnificent depiction could have been faithfully re-created on the Bayreuth
stage in 1876. The large oil painting, together with Illustration 8, are reproduced
by kind permission of Cornelia von Bodenhausen.

Stadtmuseum in Worms. Cornelius was a member of the Reichstag right through to
1918 and he and Maximilian were ennobled as barons in 1886. His passion for art
was matched by scarcely less enthusiasm for hunting. The two came together in
November 1903 at his hunting lodge on the Kühkopf island in the Rhine when fourteen
fellow enthusiasts for the chase, who included Prince Heinrich of Prussia and Nicholas
II, last Tsar of Russia, banqueted in a panelled hall on whose walls the five Hoffmanns
were displayed. One wonders whether anyone regretted the absence of any depiction of
the hunt at which Siegfried became the principal victim. The paintings remained in the
hunting lodge until 1961 when Siegfried von Heyl sold the island to the Land Hessen
(which demolished the lodge in 1978), after which they were taken to the Schlößchen
in Worms.

Meticulously researched though Dr Bauer's account is, it jumps too swiftly from
March 1995, when he first urged the Richard-Wagner-Stiftung to buy the paintings from
the Baroness, to their eventual acquisition by the Richard Wagner Museum in 2003.
He is mysteriously silent about two further large *Ring* paintings by Hoffmann which
have remained at the Schlößchen.

In the summer of 2004, while I was in the final stages of choosing illustrations for my book *Wagner and the Art of the Theatre* (2006), a good friend asked whether I was aware of some *Ring* paintings by Josef Hoffmann which he believed were still in Worms and in all probability unpublished. That friend was the art historian Simon Reynolds, who just happened to be married to Beata von Heyl, daughter of the Baroness. The story, so far as he knew, was that while the sale-to-Bayreuth negotiations remained stalled in the mid-1990s, the Hoffmanns had been given by the Baroness (who died in 2004) to her son-in-law, Baron Heinrich von Bodenhausen, who was married to her other daughter, Cornelia. I immediately wrote to von Bodenhausen, who received my enquiries with great friendliness and filled out the little I had been able to piece together about Bauer's identification of the pictures and their whereabouts. He also sent me photographs of five of them. (Bauer had already published images of three of them in an article on Gustav Mahler and Alfred Roller in the *Jahrbuch der Bayerischen Akademie der Schönen Künste 1997*, pp. 55-95.)

Von Bodenhausen told me he had sold five Hoffmanns to the Richard Wagner Museum on 8 April 2003 and that they were already there. Two further paintings were still in the Schlößchen with his wife (from whom he was separated). I subsequently learnt that the Baroness had gifted all the paintings to her son-in-law as part of the separation settlement. Von Bodenhausen told me that the two still at the Schlößchen had been promised as a gift to the Museum. Maybe I might like to come to Worms and take the pictures to Bayreuth in person, where the Museum's director, Dr Sven Friedrich, would be able to answer any further questions I might have?

This was exciting news indeed. Cornelia confirmed that she did indeed have the two paintings and sent me colour photographs of them. It was quite plain that she had no intention of parting with them. The Museum, for its part, confirmed that there were indeed seven original Hoffmanns and that they were safe, but could not tell me more as 'the whole transaction is not yet completed'. I also sought clarification from Dr Bauer himself. In his reply (which I received on 11 February 2005) he mentioned only five paintings. They were being restored for the Wahnfried Museum and he hoped would be unveiled in a special exhibition there, probably not before 2006, at which time he would publish a full account of his discovery. I readily agreed to his request that I should myself not publish anything in *Wagner and the Art of the Theatre* other than the barest facts about the paintings, which was what I did. But there seemed no reason why, if Cornelia were willing, I should not enhance my book jacket with the first-ever publication of one of her two Hoffmanns. I chose the depiction of Siegmund brandishing Nothung at the end of the first act of *Die Walküre*, this being the perfect counterpoint to my front-cover picture of Siegfried reforging the sword with a steam hammer in Chéreau's 1976 Bayreuth centenary production.

Cornelia very kindly gave her permission, while her son Henrik photographed it for me, as also the second picture which is of Loge and Wotan capturing Alberich in the Nibelheim Scene of *Das Rheingold*. I remain immensely grateful to them both. It was actually Henrik who had first discovered all the paintings. He had been staying with his grandmother in the Schlößchen for three years (1990-93) and stumbled across them while clearing a space in the huge cellars in preparation for a farewell party.

It seems that there can be only one reason why Bauer has omitted any mention of the two important Schlößchen paintings, namely that their ownership is still in dispute. Let us hope that it will soon be swiftly and amicably resolved.[1]

---

1. As at May 2023 the paintings remain at the Schlößchen.

Part Two

Arts of Interpretation

Illustration 1: The Vienna Court Opera with horse-tram, c. 1900.

Chapter Four

Tristan und Isolde, Vienna 1903

'Wie hör' ich das Licht!'[1] Gustav Mahler and Alfred Roller's abrogation of Wahnfried

Cosima Wagner, keeper of the Bayreuth shrine after the Master's death in 1883, hasn't enjoyed a good press. 'Madame Wagner', said Bernard Shaw,

> is a clever stage manager; but one of the faults of her qualities is to conceive a dramatic representation as a series of tableaux vivants, and to invent attitudes for people instead of continuous and natural action, the result being that artists get stuck for ten minutes at a time into poses that become ridiculous after ten seconds.[2]

---

1. Source: Unpublished lecture for the Oxford conference, 'Wagner 1900', April 2018. The conference was organized by Anna Stoll Knecht at Jesus College, Oxford, 9-11 April 2018.
2. 21 July 1894, review of *Lohengrin* in Dan H. Laurence (ed.), *Shaw's Music* (London: Bodley Head, 1989), vol. 3, p. 287.

Illustration 2: The Secessionists' 'Kunsttempel' in 1899, an assertively modernist building, intended not just as an art gallery but as a Temple for the integration of the arts. The motto over the entrance reads 'Der Zeit ihre Kunst, Der Kunst ihre Freiheit' (To every age its art, to every art its freedom).

Illustration 3: The Secessionists' 1902 exhibition was planned around Max Klinger's sculpture of Beethoven. Behind it can be seen part of Alfred Roller's mural 'Die sinkende Nacht' (Nightfall), that may have been inspired by the second act of *Tristan und Isolde.*

Cosima's regimentation of the stage successfully served the idea of performance as an unchanging rite. She sought to lock the works into a visual aesthetic that was purely illustrative – imitating and reflecting in naturalistic scenery the imagery of Wagner's words and music. So total was her dedication to perfecting the nineteenth-century aesthetic of stage illusion that she could conceive of no other. She treated those who could as heretics with the power to betray everything she meant by the 'Bayreuth style'.

When Gordon Craig told her over lunch in Dresden in 1905 that the 'stage trappings at Bayreuth or anywhere else' were nothing like 'the visions his music conjured up', Cosima replied '"And what pictures do *you* see, Mr Craig?" And I described something like the wild pampas of South America, the rushing of the wind, perhaps a prairie fire and so on. When I looked at Frau Wagner I could hardly see her face, because she had turned the same colour as the table cloth, into which she seemed to be vanishing.'[3]

The progressive artistic ideas of Houston Stewart Chamberlain, a formidable member of the Wahnfried circle, were in marked contrast to his extreme social and political conservatism. Chamberlain tried to interest Cosima in the radical simplifications proposed by the Swiss theatre-artist Adolphe Appia. He hoped she might incorporate them for the forthcoming *Ring* of 1896. But Cosima had no use for an approach so openly critical of her own ideas of performance.

---

3. Edward Gordon Craig, *Index to the Story of My Days* (London: Hulton Press, 1957), p. 272.

Illustration 4: 'A tentlike room on the foreward deck of a ship, richly hung with rugs.' Set model based on the design by Angelo II Quaglio for Act One of *Tristan und Isolde* at its Munich premiere, 1865.

Gustav Mahler's challenge to Bayreuth

But elsewhere Appia found a more attentive response. Gustav Mahler, arguably the greatest Wagner conductor of his generation, had in 1897 been appointed Generalmusikdirektor of the Vienna Court Opera. In his previous posts at Budapest and Hamburg he had concerned himself with all aspects of staging. As director of the Budapest Opera his domination of every part of the production was remarked on by a certain Count Albert Apponyi:

> he governs with sovereign authority the stage, the action, the movements of the soloists and the chorus; so that a performance rehearsed and produced by him is in every way artistically complete. His eye extends over the entire production, the scenery, the machinery, the lights.[4]

Mahler had been a regular attender at Bayreuth since 1883. He knew only too well that there was life beyond Cosima's perpetuation of the 'Bayreuth style'. How to achieve this was another matter. Mahler was a voracious reader, especially of anything that could have a bearing on his work. So it is more than likely he would have come across Appia's principal work, *Die Musik und die Inszenierung* (Music and Stage Production), which was published in Vienna in 1899, not least because it includes an appendix

---

4. Cited in Kurt Blaukopf (ed.) with Zoltan Roman, *Mahler: A Documentary Study* (Oxford/ New York: Oxford University Press, 1976), p. 183.

Illustration 5: Act One of *Tristan und Isolde* as imagined by the Vienna Opera's scenic artist Carlo Brioschi, 1883.

Illustration 6: Gustav Mahler, drawn by Emil Orlik, 1902.

Illustration 7: Alfred Roller, 1908.

on the staging of *Tristan und Isolde*. And if he'd missed that, he could have seen the extracts from the book that were published in December 1900 in Vienna's leading cultural journal, the *Wiener Rundschau*, under the title 'Das Licht und die Inszenierung'.[5]

Its thesis that in opera only the music should be allowed to determine the staging struck home. Mahler was convinced by Appia's contention that the nineteenth-century *Illusionsbühne*, meaning a stage aspiring to mimic reality,

---

5. Adolphe Appia, *Die Musik und die Inszenierung* (Munich: Bruckmann, 1899). Extracts from this as 'Das Licht und die Inszenierung' in *Wiener Rundschau 4*, no. 24 (15 December 1900), pp. 422-28. For a fuller discussion of Appia, see 'Reinventing Wagner after Hitler', Chapter 6 in this book.

had to be replaced by a new *Andeutungsbühne,* a stage on which everything should be suggested rather than shown.

Mahler was well aware of the widespread movement for theatre reform that had powerfully stirred in the 1890s (especially in Paris, Munich and Berlin). By the end of the century it had begun to take wing in straight theatre. Opera, by comparison, was a cumbersome battleship, not easily turned. While in Hamburg in the 1890s, he'd told Natalie Bauer-Lechner that if he became opera director in Vienna:

> there would be damned little emphasis on sets and costumes. ... I'd force the misguided public and its jaded taste along quite a different path. It would be a blessing if much more – in fact, practically everything – could be left to the listener's fantasy and powers of imagination. In this respect, I'd like to take Munich's Shakespeare theatre as a model. They would really get to *hear* the thing with me, which they haven't done yet'.[6]

It was Mahler's good fortune to have arrived in Vienna (1897) in the middle of an artistic ferment antagonistic to the conservative values of the bourgeoisie. He soon established a close relationship with the artists of the Vienna Secession. This was a group that on 3 April 1897, five days before his initial appointment as conductor at the Court Opera, broke away from the stranglehold of the official Academy. They established themselves as the *Vereinigung bildender Künstler Österreichs* (The Association of Austrian Artists).[7] Mahler's relationship with them didn't blossom immediately but only on his meeting with Alma Schindler in 1901.

Alma was the daughter of Emil Jakob Schindler, a highly regarded landscape painter. Her own youthful accomplishments included painting, sculpture and musical composition. After Schindler's death her mother married another painter, Carl Moll, who was the second president of the Secession (1899-1901). It was at his house on 7 November 1901 that Mahler first met the 22-year-old Alma, and within months they were married (on 9 March 1902).

The Viennese Secessionists and the 'total work of art'

The director of the Imperial Opera was plunged into the very centre of the new movement in art. Alma reports that its leading practitioners, most particularly Moll, Gustav Klimt, Alfred Roller and Koloman Moser 'vied with one another to be his teacher'.[8] For his part Mahler had much to offer the Secessionists, not least because their programme sought to dissolve boundaries between the arts. A central part of their aesthetic was that their exhibitions were not just pictures hung on walls but

---

6. Cited in Natalie Bauer-Lechner, *Recollections of Gustav Mahler,* trans. Dika Newlin, ed. Peter Franklin (London: Faber and Faber, 1980), p. 93.
7. Henry-Louis de La Grange, *Gustav Mahler,* trans. Johanna Harwood, Meredith Oakes et al. (Oxford: Oxford University Press, vol. 2, 1995), p. 503.
8. Alma Mahler, *Gustav Mahler: Memories and Letters,* ed. Donald Mitchell, trans. Basil Creighton, 3rd edition (London: John Murray, 1973), p. 160.

Illustration 8: Alfred Roller's design for the beginning of Act One, Vienna, 1903.

were *Gesamtkunstwerke*, 'total works of art'. They also built for themselves a boldly geometric *Kunsttempel*, designed by Josef Olbrich after a sketch by Klimt, which was completed in 1898.

In this modernist temple, it was planned that the exhibits, events and even musical performances should make a 'total' experience for the visitor. The Fourteenth Secession Exhibition, organized by Alfred Roller (April-June 1902), was focussed on Max Klinger's monumental new sculpture of Beethoven. It was set in a shrine-like enclosure by the architect Josef Hoffmann.[9] (Mahler was invited to collaborate in this Beethoven-Fest: at the opening of the exhibition he conducted his own arrangement for six trombones of a passage from the choral movement of the Ninth Symphony.)

Behind Klinger's rather monstrously enthroned, *Sturm und Drang* Beethoven, at the left on the upper wall, one can just about see the quasi-abstract mural painted by Roller, *Die sinkende Nacht* (Nightfall). Is it too fanciful to imagine that the mural may have been inspired by the 'O sink hernieder, Nacht der Liebe' love-duet in the second act of *Tristan*? If so, it would have been an anticipation of the stage designs Roller was shortly to prepare for Mahler.[10] On the opposite wall, Beethoven was facing a complementary

---

9. Illustrations in Peter Vergo, *Art in Vienna 1898-1918* (London: Phaidon Press, 1975), pp. 67 and 70. This Josef Hoffmann is not to be confused with his namesake, the artist whom Wagner commissioned to design the *Ring* at Bayreuth in 1876 – see 'Designs on the *Ring*', Chapter 3 in this book.

10. It is, I believe, highly likely that Roller, like Mahler, as mentioned above, would have already been aware of Appia's ideas. Roller's archive in the Österreichisches Theater-museum, Vienna, includes three letters to him from Appia, dating from 1907, all of which are concerned with theatre reform and ideas for staging *Parsifal*: Evan Baker and Oskar Pausch, *Das Archiv Alfred Roller* (Vienna: Böhlau, 1994).

Illustration 9: A preliminary sketch by Roller for the end of Act One, Vienna, 1903.

Illustration 10: Photograph of the end of Act One of Roller's *Tristan* as performed in Vienna, 1943.

Illustration 11: Erik
Schmedes as Tristan,
Vienna, 1903.

Illustration 12: Anna von
Mildenburg as Isolde,
Vienna, 1903.

depiction of *Der werdende Tag* (Daybreak) by Adolf Böhm. It is hard not to feel that the title isn't also an allusion to the night versus day antagonism that is so central to *Tristan*. Roller had only recently discovered, and been swept away by, *Tristan und Isolde*. He would have seen it in the traditional-style performances under Mahler's baton at the Imperial Opera. Act One would have been an interpretation by the theatre's leading scenic artist, Carlo Brioschi of the opera's 1865 premiere in Munich and of Cosima's even more luxuriously caparisoned Bayreuth production from 1886.

Roller had hated Brioschi's settings and been fired to make sketches of his own. These he showed to Mahler. So impressed was the conductor that, recognizing the 'true visual expression' of the Wagnerian drama, and despite Roller's total lack of stage experience, he commissioned him to design new settings for *Tristan*.[11] For Roller this proved to be as decisive a turning point as it was for Mahler and, indeed, for the future course of opera production.[12]

While wishing, in his opera house, to dispense with the pictorial literalism of the late nineteenth century, Mahler had so far lacked a collaborator, someone who could help him effect on the deeply conservative operatic stage a comparable revolution to that already under way in the spoken theatre. In Alfred Roller he had found his man.

Born in Moravia in 1864, Roller had studied painting at the Vienna Akademie der bildenden Künste. A founder-member of the Secession, he became a co-editor of its journal *Ver Sacrum* (Sacred Spring) in 1898, and replaced Carl Moll as president in 1902. Roller's interest in spatial arrangement had showed itself in the rooms he designed for the Secession exhibitions. It was to be but a short step from here to his discovery of a new medium in the three-dimensional arena of the stage. His and Mahler's common point of departure was the elimination of anything visual that didn't relate to their understanding of the music. This didn't mean the rejection of pictorial imagery but rather its re-creation in *spatial* terms. The stage, said Roller, dealt not with *pictures*, but with space.

The romantic realism of the Vienna Opera's scenic style created by Carlo Brioschi up to 1886, and thereafter by his son Anton, was to be superseded by simpler images. All the scenic essentials specified by Wagner would still be there, but in stylized form. Roller later recalled that Mahler had welcomed 'a stage on which everything is only

---

11. De La Grange, *Mahler,* vol. 2, p. 561.
12. See: Oswald Georg Bauer, '"daß der Ausdruck Eindruck werde." Gustav Mahler und Alfred Roller. Die Reform der Wiener Wagner-Szene' in *Jahrbuch der Bayerischen Akademie der Schönen Künste*, Band 11, 1997, pp. 55-95.

intimated'.[13] The aim would no longer be the creation of a peep-show illusion, but of a functional stage-space animated by the performers. Roller and Mahler were set on using the latest technology in order to paint the stage with light rather than pigment. The Opera's lighting installation, dating from 1887, was therefore improved during the *Tristan* rehearsals.[14] Light became a principal agent in the search for a visual stylization and for symbols which, in activating the audience's imagination, would deepen the musicality of its response. The dominant colour of a scene or whole act could determine its significance in the dramatic structure of the whole. The key to everything was Wagner's music, not his visual taste. Mahler's first principle – which, of course, was also Appia's – was constant: 'Steht alles in der Partitur' (It's

Illustration 13 and 14: Alfred Roller's sketches for the beginning and ending of Act Two, Vienna 1903.

all in the score).[15] But however much Mahler was indebted to the libertarian thrust of the Secessionists, he was wary of the least whiff of theatrical theory or of anything doctrinaire. He didn't want to hear his productions described as 'Secessionist' but simply as serving their composers faithfully. Thus in September 1903 he is quoted as saying:

> we want to make the *light* serve the theatre in all its grades, nuances and degrees of strength. … But the matter does not end with the lighting; the whole of modern art has a part to play on the stage. Modern art, I say, not the Secession. What matters is the conjunction of all the arts. There is no future in

---

13. Alfred Roller, 'Mahler und die Inszenierung', *Musikblätter des Anbruch*, vol. 2 (1920) (Mahler issue), cited in Peter Heyworth, *Otto Klemperer*, vol. 1 (Cambridge: Cambridge University Press, 1983), p. 27.

14. De La Grange, *Mahler,* vol. 2, p. 577 n.

15. Cited in Heyworth, *Klemperer,* vol. 1, pp. 27-28.

Illustration 15: Alfred Roller's colour-wash drawing for Act Three, the 'Burggarten' (castle garden) shaded by one huge lime tree.

the old standard clichés; modern art must extend to costumes, props, every-thing that can revitalize a work of art.[16]

Tristan und Isolde, Vienna 1903: 'Wie hör' ich das Licht!'

From the surviving pictures it isn't immediately apparent why Mahler's production of *Tristan und Isolde* struck its contemporaries as so extraordinary. Roller's settings provided every pictorial image specified by Wagner, creating credible locations on board ship, in the garden of Isolde's house at night and at Tristan's castle in Kareol. What surprised audiences was that these settings made no attempt at imitating the composer's 1865 production in Munich (Illustration 4) or Cosima's later Bayreuth staging of 1886.

Roller brilliantly simplified such over-upholstered stagings. At the beginning of the first act the awnings are not just decorative but have a dramatic purpose.

They cocoon Isolde in her prison beneath the deck of the stern. They are the visual expression of her sense of being brutally packaged so that she can scarcely breathe, a victim, contained and wrapped up for delivery to King Mark. When Isolde cries for 'Luft! Luft!' (Air! Air!), the awnings begin to open up along with her mounting determination to take action by confronting the Tristan who has betrayed her. It is a transition from the darkness of her inner world to the challenge of dealing with the odious Day: the upper, bright deck is for Tristan, the lower, claustrophobic dark quarters for Isolde.

---

16. Interview in *Illustriertes Wiener Extrablatt*, 9 September 1903, cited in Blaukopf, *Mahler Documentary*, p. 23.

Without any artifice, Roller's design enabled Tristan and Kurwenal to be visible to the audience while remaining totally out of sight from Isolde and Brangäne. So far as I am aware there are no photos of what this actually looked like in 1903. But how the scene looked in the Vienna revival of 1943 is clear from Illustration 10.

At the end of the act, all the sails and awnings were hoisted up and away to herald Mark's arrival, the king's red banner flapping against a bright-blue sky while a brilliant carpet for his welcome snaked out as an

Illustration 16: 'Lösche des Lichtes letzten Schein!' (Put out the light to its last flicker). Design for Act Two by Adolphe Appia, 1890s.

intrusive gash across the forestage at the feet of Tristan and Isolde. The scandal of the lovers' embrace was intensified by its being observed by the sailors, themselves unseen at the rail of the upper deck. It is not just a ship: Roller's scenery is talking about the characters' emotions. This was the first time that a stage of international renown, rather than copying the authorized version, had gone back to Wagner's score and created its own new images from it.

In 1903 the Danish heroic tenor Erik Schmedes was the Tristan, while Isolde was taken by the great Anna von Mildenburg. In the 1890s Mildenburg had been Mahler's lover when they worked together in Hamburg. Cosima Wagner had accepted his recommendation of her as an ideal Kundry for Bayreuth. And Mahler coached her for what was to become one of her most celebrated roles. The personal relationship fizzled out after Mahler had met Alma in 1901, but the artistic partnership remained undiminished. There can be no question that she was a powerful singing actress in the mould of Wagner's Wilhelmine Schröder-Devrient – or perhaps in more recent times Maria Callas. Erwin Stein described how Mildenburg conveyed every gradation of Isolde's 'love and hate, darkness and fury, sensitivity and spitefulness, passion and despair, exaltation and grief'.[17] In retirement, she became a renowned teacher. From her fascinating little book (1936) of guidance for singers undertaking the principal roles in *Tristan und Isolde,* we can get some idea about how she would have sung and acted Isolde for Mahler: her instructions are pretty dogmatic, though her aim was that every movement should be rooted in the drama expressed by the music.[18]

---

17. Cited by Karin Martensen in the programme for 'Scenes from Wagner's *Tristan und Isolde*' presented in the Sheldonian Theatre, Oxford, as part of the 2018 conference 'Wagner 1900'.

18. Anna Bahr-Mildenburg, *Tristan und Isolde: Darstellung des Werkes aus dem Geiste der Dichtung und Musik* (Leipzig: Musikwissenschaftlicher Verlag, 1936). A typical instance

In the second and third acts the significant scenic innovations were the 'built' solidity of the masonry (for the tower, steps and castle at Kareol) and a drastic pruning of the customary foliage. But what everyone was talking about was not the scenery but the way it was lit. It was Roller's new-found skill in painting with light that was the major breakthrough. For him this was a natural development of his interest in the effects of changing light, manifest in a series of paintings of a single landscape view in different seasons and at different times of day that he showed at the Secession in 1900.[19] There could scarcely have been a better subject for Roller's stage debut than an opera ruled so pervasively by the symbolism of Day and Night.

What was particularly striking was Roller's use of colour symbolism. As we have seen, there was an almost garish orange-yellow tonality in Act One for the hateful realm of Day. For Act Two there was a deep-violet velvety darkness, and for the long reckoning of Act Three a dull autumnal grey. Roller's sketches for Act Two contrast the torch and the starry sky at the beginning of the act with at its end the unwelcome dawning of Day. Here is the impression of a critic, Ernst Decsey, who was there:

> Out of the Prelude … the blue night rose mysterious and this night was not the hitherto invariable, obvious, static picture, but breathed and trembled like the orchestra, the garden came alive around the lovers, getting darker or lighter with straying moonbeams and drifting shadows.[20]

Towards the end of the act, when King Mark and cruel Day break in on the lovers,

> it wasn't the usual idiotic stage dawn that filled the sky but an excruciating greyness that made you shiver at the very sight of it.[21]

For Julius Korngold, father of the famous composer Erich Korngold, Roller's Act Three was 'painted *Tristan* music', the colours suggesting 'weariness, illness, ruin, and imminent death'.[22] Roller's sketches for this act include a pale image with silver birches in the foreground and a stronger one dominated by a large tree. It is not clear from the contemporary reports which setting was actually used, but it would most probably have been the second one. The composer Egon Wellesz – subsequently a much-loved Oxford don – remarked:

---

from Isolde's very first scene: at 'Hört meinen Willen, / zagende Winde!' (Hear my will, you timorous winds!) 'gebietend den rechten Arm in die Höhe, sehr stramm in der Haltung, bei "heran" eine weitausholende Gebärde des rechten Armes, bei "Wettergetös" das gleiche mit dem linken Arm.' (Raising the right arm aloft, the body erect and tensed, at 'heran' a commanding gesture with the right arm, at 'Wettergetös' the same gesture with the left arm), n. 17, p. 37.

19. De La Grange, *Mahler*, vol. 2, p. 573 n.
20. Emil Lucka, cited in De La Grange, *Mahler*, vol. 2, p. 573.
21. Ernst Decsey, cited in Norman Lebrecht (ed.), *Mahler Remembered* (London: Faber, 1987), p. 266.
22. Cited in De La Grange, *Mahler*, vol. 2, pp. 580 and 574.

A barren, desolate landscape just as in the music. Behind the low rampart one imagined the sea. Never had a scene made such a profound impression on me.[23]

Quite how Roller, unschooled in stage technology, learnt how to manipulate the lights we don't yet know, but the results were sensational. 'Untiringly,' said Emil Lucka, 'he carried out his tests, moving from the stage to the stalls, from the stalls to the gallery, experimenting with screens, coloured discs, light-intensities, altering, improving, dealing in nuances.'[24] Roller was among the very first practitioners of *Lichtregie* – the use of the lighting console as a principal agent in the staging of opera. Among his discoveries was the dynamic use of light in every grade of intensity, including crescendos and decrescendos between dark and light.

The low levels of intensity to which, when dramatically appropriate, Roller was prepared to reduce the lighting (as in Act Two of *Tristan*) were much complained about – the general custom being a relatively high and constant level of illumination. But what would the Viennese have thought about Appia's extreme depiction of Act Two in 1896? It was this drawing that would very likely have been in Roller's mind.

The costumes were also Roller's work. Roller was, at Mahler's express instruction, the first head of stage design to be entrusted with scenery, costumes and lighting, responsibilities formerly divided between three people. For the most part his costumes were traditional, if not untouched by the Secessionist love of patterning. We have to accept that the decorative impulse in his aesthetic was never entirely comfortable with Mahler's more ascetic preference. As the surviving photos show Mildenburg in a relatively simple gown, we can assume that it was Mahler's preference – and, indeed, also Mildenburg's – that here prevailed.[25] She had asked Roller for 'a costume without decoration … made from a light grey cloth, combined with effective embroidery, so that any jewellery can be omitted'.[26]

Mahler was never an uncritical admirer of the Secessionists. His visual sense was closer to the architect Adolf Loos' philosophy: 'Lack of ornament is a sign of spiritual strength!'[27] Certainly Loos, a scourge of the Secessionists, was openly scornful of what he considered the decorative indulgence of Roller's settings: 'There are too many coffers around. Nicely arranged. The carpet is Rudniker (Prague). I've used them too. For the entrance hall. All those cushions look nice.'[28]

23. Egon and Emmy Wellesz, *Egon Wellesz: Leben und Werk*, ed. Franz Endler (Vienna and Hamburg: Zsolnay, 1981), p. 25.

24. Cited in Blaukopf, *Mahler Documentary*, p. 173.

25. See Illustration 13.

26. Cited by Karin Martensen in the programme for the 2018 Oxford performance of 'Scenes from *Tristan und Isolde*'. In a contemporaneous portrait by Franz Matsch, Mildenburg is depicted (as Isolde) in a modishly fashionable gown whose gilded patterning, although designed by Roller, was far more typical of Klimt (illustrated in Blaukopf, *Mahler Documentary*, plate 178). This was painterly fantasy and not what she wore on the stage.

27. Adolf Loos (1908), cited in Blaukopf, *Mahler Documentary*, p. 174.

28. Adolf Loos, *Trotzdem* (1900-30) (Innsbruck: Brenner, 1931), cited in De La Grange, *Mahler*, vol. 2, p. 585.

The production was a huge and immediate success. Dissenting voices were in the minority. Roller was variously reproached for imperfect sight lines, for failing to integrate the singers into the settings, for creating too much visual beauty and for 'his orgies of darkness'. The critic Robert Hirschfeld complained that Mildenburg's 'subtle pantomime' went for nothing because of what he considered the prevalent gloom.[29] Siegfried Wagner, attending the premiere on 21 February, also moaned about the lighting, later giving Ernst Decsey the predictable Bayreuth line: 'My father mounted the production of *Tristan* himself in Munich, so I'm afraid that's it and that's how it will have to stay.'[30] The singers were mostly well received and the praise for Mahler's conducting was universal.

The wider significance of the production as a 'total work of art' was recognized by the more perceptive critics. Max Graf wrote that Wagner might have been astonished that his vision had inspired such an imaginative response from the world of art, but also shocked that the artist appeared to be wishing to prevail in his own right. While nothing could have been further from Roller's ambition, Graf's review does point up just how iconoclastic Roller's contribution was generally considered to be.[31] The idea that a scenic artist could make an *original* contribution to the performance of an opera was revolutionary, and was immediately recognized as such.

This *Tristan und Isolde* was given 20 times during Mahler's directorship and became a staple of the Vienna Court Opera. Indeed, it was fated to become a classic that was performed more than 180 times up to Furtwängler's wartime revival in 1943. This was to be its last outing (six performances) as most of the theatre, together with its scenery and costumes, were destroyed by Allied bombing in March 1945.

Having discovered his scenic collaborator, Mahler went on to apply the Wagnerian principle of a unified production, rooted in the music, to everything he performed. Roller describes how Mahler only agreed to his designs for *Don Giovanni* (21 December 1905) 'after long reflection had convinced him of their relevance to the work's musical shape'.[32] The novelty was the square towers at either side of the stage near the front which remained throughout the opera and 'between which the various changes of scenery took place'.[33] The towers were Roller's solution to the perennial problem in *Don Giovanni* of effecting a large number of scene changes fast enough to avoid unnecessary breaks in the music. Thus the operatic debut of a set with permanent (though also changeable) features. This invention of the idea of a unifying, multi-purpose, non-naturalistic scenic artefact capable of symbolizing the drama as a whole, was to have a huge influence on Mahler and Roller's successors in twentieth-century stage production.

---

29. De La Grange, *Mahler*, vol 2, pp. 573-85.

30. Ernst Decsey (1911), cited in Lebrecht, *Mahler Remembered*, p. 267.

31. Max Graf, 'Der Sezessionistische Tristan', *Hamburger Nachrichten*, 15 March 1903, cited in De La Grange, *Mahler*, vol. 2, pp. 583-84.

32. Cited in Heyworth, *Klemperer*, vol. 1, pp. 27-28.

33. Bruno Walter, *Theme and Variations*, trans. James S. Galston (London: Hamish Hamilton, 1947), pp. 158-59.

Illustration 17: Sketch by Roller for the final scene of *Das Rheingold*, 1903.

First steps to a new *Ring,* Vienna 1905-07

Sketches in the Theatre Collection of the Austrian National Library show that Roller went on almost immediately after *Tristan* to plan for a new *Ring.* (Vienna's Bayreuth-style production had remained virtually unchanged since its creation in 1879.)[34] The working sketches and their realization in the finished productions of *Das Rheingold* (23 January 1905) and *Die Walküre* (4 February 1907) show, on the one hand, Roller the painter wanting to re-create nature in the theatre and, on the other, Roller the stage designer seeking simplification and visual drama. One of Roller's criteria was to eliminate anything likely to come across as puerile or risible. Hence Alberich's transformations into giant serpent and then toad were masked in a gloom of vapour and black-velvet drapes, while the previous wooden 'rainbow bridge' was abandoned altogether – as the curtain fell, the gods were moving slowly towards an optical rainbow projection.

Like Wagner's movement-director Richard Fricke, Roller believed that it was always better to appeal to the imagination rather than risk offence to the intellect. In Hunding's hut, the light came just from the hearth and a single torch on the right-hand wall (Illustration 18). Roller re-sited the door so that when it flew open the moonlight streamed in diagonally and it was *only* at that moment that there was enough light for the facial similarity of the twins to be apparent.

---

34. De La Grange, *Mahler,* vol. 2 (French edition), (Paris: Fayard 1983/91), p. 541.

Much of the criticism against the low levels of lighting was on the grounds that the singers' expressions and gestures went for nothing. For all the efforts Mahler would have made, and for all the power and artistry of the vocal performances, characterization and acting came across less strongly than the sheerly visual drama.[35] The problem of the actor's integration into the setting remained imperfectly solved.

The debut of the art of the director

What Roller and Mahler had shown is that fidelity to the protean spirit of a dramatist's work is more artistically fruitful than fidelity to the letter of his intentions. The right to interrogate a work of genius and come up with answers undreamt of by its creator was established once and for all. It marked the birth, for the opera stage, of the shocking idea that production is more than the realization of the composer's blueprint and can be creative in its own right. As already suggested, the special authority of Mahler and Roller as iconoclasts who were themselves creators of genius, undoubtedly played a major part in winning acceptance for what was then a revolutionary idea in opera production – though right down to today this is far from universal. It is perhaps remarkable that the proving ground should have been Wagner, the only composer whose 'afterlife' came to be so zealously protected by his heirs. The Vienna productions were the first effective challenge to its hegemony.

Mahler himself believed that the disciplined simplicity of his last collaboration with Roller, Gluck's *Iphigénie en Aulide* (18 March 1907), was their best work, a view shared by Bruno Walter and Lilli Lehmann.[36] Unfortunately there appears to be no illustration of this, though Roller's design for the 1909 Dresden premiere of Strauss' *Elektra* will typify his almost Appian response to classical antiquity.

Roller stayed on to complete the new *Ring* with Mahler's successor, Felix von Weingartner, but the magic had fled. Feeling himself undervalued by Weingartner, Roller resigned his Opera post in May 1909 and took over the directorship of the Kunstgewerbeschule (School for Applied Arts). He went on to do important theatre work with, inter alia, the Burgtheater, Max Reinhardt in Berlin and the Vienna Opera (1918-34), where he returned to design productions for Strauss' operas. In 1920 he was a co-founder of the Salzburg Festival, and in 1934 made a belated Bayreuth debut in designing sets and costumes for Heinz Tietjen's production of *Parsifal*. Roller often reverted to a pictorial, decorative style – as in his famous designs for the premiere of *Der Rosenkavalier* in Munich in 1911. But the fastidious, elegant efficiency of his designs, their truth to the musical drama he had so momentously developed in his best work with Mahler, never deserted him.

---

35. De La Grange, *Mahler*, vol. 2 (French edition), p. 1040 ff.
36. *Selected Letters of Gustav Mahler*, ed. Knud Martner, trans. Eithne Wilkins, Ernst Kaiser and Bill Hopkins (London: Faber, 1979), p. 300; Walter, *Theme and Variations*, p. 158; Lilli Lehmann, *My Path through Life*, trans. Alice Benedict Seligman (London: G.P. Putnam's Sons, 1914), p. 388.

Illustration 18: Sketch by Roller for Act One of *Die Walküre*, 1904.

Illustration 19: Roller's chalk sketch for Richard Strauss's *Elektra*, 1909.

Illustration 1: Patrice Chéreau's centennial staging of the *Ring* at Bayreuth: the Rhinedaughters (Ilse Gramatzki, Yoko Kawahara and Adelheid Krauss) soliciting Alberich (Zoltán Kelemen) under the shadow of designer Richard Peduzzi's ominous dam across the river. The conductor was Pierre Boulez.

Chapter Five

Damming the Rhine[1]

Patrice Chéreau's *Ring* at Bayreuth 1976

This essay for *The Times Literary Supplement* was written in response to the publication of Hans Mayer's *Richard Wagner in Bayreuth 1876-1976* (Stuttgart: Belser, 1976) and to Patrice Chéreau and Pierre Boulez's now legendary 1976 *Ring* at Bayreuth. The production was intensely controversial, with tussles breaking out in the Festspielhaus and noisy interruptions even bringing the performance to a halt. My wife Jill and I were not uninvolved. We had found ourselves sitting next to a beautiful woman who introduced herself as Violeta, wife of the renowned American tenor Jess Thomas who was singing Siegfried in *Götterdämmerung*. At the very end of that opera a disaffected man in the row in front of us began to blow piercingly on one of the whistles that were prominently on sale outside the theatre. When I leant forward to remonstrate with him we got into a heated exchange ('I am German

1. Source: *Times Literary Supplement*, 10 June 1977, pp. 707-08.

and we are a democracy so I can do as I like') and fisticuffs were only averted by Jill and Violeta's intervention. We and Jess soon became friends, Jess enthusiastically accepting my invitation to talk to the students at the Bayreuth International Youth Festival where I was giving the English-language Wagner seminars. As word got about, participants from all the other seminars abandoned them, crowded into the room and were enthralled by Jess.

* * *

Wagner has always had trouble with the French, as witness what have probably been the two most sensational of the many theatrical rows occasioned by his work. The first was the 1861 Paris performance of *Tannhäuser* when Wagner's refusal to supply the conventional second- rather than first-act ballet incurred the fury of the Jockey Club members. These connoisseurs, from whose opera glasses it was said that the dancers' tights withheld no secrets, were no more in the habit of appearing at the Opéra until the second act than the *premières danseuses* themselves, for the very good reason that they dined out together until that time.

The second major scandal was the 1976 Bayreuth centenary performances of the *Ring* as produced by Patrice Chéreau, a 31-year-old Frenchman with only two previous operatic stagings to his name – *Les Contes d'Hoffmann* and *Il turco in Italia*. The Rhinemaidens as whores, Wotan as a crazed Victorian inventor sporting Wagner's own brocade dressing-gown, and Siegfried in a dinner-jacket sufficed to create uproar on the sacred Green Hill and a demand for tickets only exceeded by that for this year's second showing.

When one recalls the Francophobia of Wagner's 1871 poem 'To the German Army before Paris' (which called for the total devastation of France) and the hysterical jingoism of his satire on the besieged communards 'Eine Kapitulation', supposedly in the Aristophanian mode (for which he suggested a setting in the style of Offenbach), not to mention his Bakunin-inspired conception of the firing of Valhalla as the cremation of Paris, it would be understandable to see Chéreau as the instrument of French revenge. Was it that, or was it just a particularly masochistic instalment of the atonement programme entered into by the Wagner grandsons when they revived the festival in 1951? Whether Wolfgang knew what he was getting in Chéreau, we may never know. But there can be no doubt that he needed sensation, that he got it and that he was by no means displeased.

The official commemorative booklet of the centenary festival, recently published as an appetizer for the 1977 festival, triumphantly reprints a selection of the wickedest things that have been said about Bayreuth over the years. The 1976 offerings are especially excitable. 'A curse and destruction to you and the French *Ring*-team', said one letter to Herr Wagner. 'What you have done to Richard Wagner's legacy is a crime. One ought to put all those concerned in front of a firing-squad.' Elsewhere, the booklet prints the President of the Federal Republic's confession, made at the celebrations, that he personally was no Wagnerite and felt no compulsion to profess his faith in Bayreuth. Yes, Wagner was a great composer, but not the only one: 'Mussorgsky's music is certainly as bold and *novateur* as Wagner's – and as a poet Pushkin, too, can stand comparison with Wagner,' Walter Scheel told the devotees, going on to give a particularly vicious twist to the dagger in the wound: 'Again, Verdi's great operas are on a par with those of Richard Wagner.' After *diese Töne*, what could Herr Wagner do but abandon his own prepared speech and call for the music of *Die Meistersinger* to demolish such blasphemy?

Paris has not always got Wagner as wrong as the claque who in 1876 booed the overture to Weber's *Der Freischütz* under the impression that it was the funeral march from *Götterdämmerung*. Indeed the French have shown a passion and flair for Wagner from which have stemmed critiques of his work no less powerful than those of Nietzsche. They have been as evident in the burlesque of adulation – 'On va à Bayreuth', says Albert Lavignac at the outset of *Le Voyage artistique à Bayreuth* (1897), 'comme on veut, à pied, à cheval, en voiture, à bicyclette, en chemin de fer, et le vrai pèlerin devrait y aller à genoux' – as in the response of men like Berlioz, Baudelaire, Catulle Mendès, Debussy, and now Boulez, who did his own fine thing down below in the Festspielhaus pit while Chéreau was about some other business on the boards above.

Paris' rejection of the young Wagner in 1839-42 gave him from the outset an inside appreciation of the alien operation of the Gallic muse. That essential difference he was to characterize shortly afterwards in *Tannhäuser*, where the hero flees the sirens and erotic exhaustion of the Venusberg, awakening to wholesome new life in the pastoral German landscape with its shepherds, shawms, pilgrims and wayside shrine. It was the Paris of Louis Philippe, where art was one more commodity, which brought home to Wagner E.T.A. Hoffmann's insight that art in a bourgeois society had at all costs to avoid that which was required of it, namely diversion, decoration and ornament. Thus, as Hans Mayer points out in his new book on Richard Wagner in Bayreuth,[2] Tannhäuser's contribution to the song contest is a *coup* – a counter-art, under the immediate provocation of Wolfram's romantic traditionalism.

That part of the French response to Wagner that was not drugging itself with his potions was swift to subject the *Gesamtcosmos* to the chill wind of strictly conditional belief, and to a scepticism that refused to take Old Klingsor on his own terms. So while the enraptured Guillaume Lekeu fainted during the Prelude to *Tristan* and had to be carried from the total darkness of the Festspielhaus, Chabrier, once he had recovered from a tearful outburst at the same performance, was cheered by the discovery that the sublime music furnished ideal themes for a set of bumptious quadrilles.

Hardly the kind of thing to draw a smile from Frau Cosima, bent as she was after Wagner's death in 1883 on consolidating the Germanic core of his works, defending them against their mutilation and old-style romanticization at the hands of other opera houses.

The story of the fate suffered by Wagner's works after his death in his very own theatre has been told before. But the centenary has produced a crop of new studies, among them Professor Mayer's, which draws on extensive, newly available, documentation that

---

2. Hans Mayer, *Richard Wagner in Bayreuth 1876-1976* (Stuttgart: Belser, 1976). An English edition, trans. Jack Zipes, is available from the same publisher.

reveals the politics and aesthetics of Bayreuth history in a new, if somewhat murky, light.[3]

Professor Mayer, however, is at some pains to absolve Cosima from much of the opprobrium that has fallen on her. He does this by insisting that 'it is historically false and hence morally unjust to equate the Bayreuth Festival system of Cosima Wagner with the concentrated reactionary ideology of the *Bayreuther Blätter* and the anti-Semitic and racial activities of people like Wolzogen, Schemann, or even Chamberlain'. The evidence itself, however, does not altogether go along with this case. For although after Wagner's death Cosima may have increasingly dissociated herself publicly from the Gobineau-*Vereinigung*, she did so largely for pragmatic reasons; the published correspondence with Chamberlain shows that if anything she became more reactionary as the years went by. She simply saw that the unabashed anti-Semitic and nationalist thrust of the Bayreuther *Kreis* – the self-appointed false guardians of the Grail (though in fact of the *wrong* Grail) who sought to turn the art of a former revolutionary into an ideological weapon for political and cultural regression – was a threat to the international revenue the festival required, and perhaps even to the artistic and spiritual values that she was dedicated to perpetuating, or at any rate embalming, at Bayreuth. Some members of the *Kreis* suspected her of being secretly un-German and cosmopolitan – after all she had been brought up in Paris among Jews, liberals, homosexuals, socialists and worse.

Thus in 1896, 20 years after the opening of Bayreuth, by which time Cosima had produced there all Wagner's mature works with the exception of *Der fliegende Holländer*, Martin Plüddemann wrote to his fellow ideologue Schemann that 'Cosima's pure French character is dangerous in that it has brought about a Bayreuth internationalism. At any rate, she is un-German from head to toe, and this will bring about the ruin of Bayreuth!'. Seen in this albeit erroneous light, one could be forgiven for believing that Cosima herself was an inside agent of the French corrective.

After a heart attack in 1906, Cosima relinquished management of the festival to her son. Siegfried had grown up in a matriarchal society against which his own operas were a transparent protest. Hans Mayer nicely suggests that 'the composer who wrote a ballad for baritones and orchestra about a "fat, greasy pancake" which becomes horrified at the sight of old women, jumps out of the frying pan and runs away, must have known what he was implying here'. The young Siegfried's notes for dramatic projects include a line from *The Magic Flute*: '*Bewahret Euch vor Weibertücken!*' (Watch

---

3. It appears that Mayer's book, which acknowledges documentation by Wolfgang Wagner's son Gottfried, was commissioned by Wolfgang as an answer to Michael Karbaum's *Studien our Geschichte der Bayreuther Festspiele* (Regensburg: Gustav Bosse, 1976). Karbaum had published correspondence and documents acutely embarrassing to Bayreuth as it sought international validation with its French centenary *Ring*. Far more subversive than Karbaum's scholarly tome had been Hans-Jürgen Syberberg's film, *Winifred Wagner und die Geschichte des Hauses Wahnfried*, which had created a sensation when aired on German television in 1975. In the film, Wolfgang's mother Winifred had talked shamelessly about her friendship with Hitler and his association with the *Festspiele*. See also Chapter 6 in this book, 'Reinventing Wagner after Hitler'.

out for women's tricks). The self-exhortation was in vain, for the protagonists of his later operas succumb, growing ever more passive as sufferers, martyrs and victims.

The wonder is that Siegfried, whose rule was still dominated by his mother (she lived on until 1930), had it in him to be even an acceptable conductor, composer, producer, administrator and all the rest of it – not that the 'acceptable' was good enough for his father, rather was it for *him* the enemy itself. Had Bayreuth then been anything but a museum – of which he was the agreeable, somewhat bemused curator – he would surely have been hopelessly inadequate.

Siegfried hated not only *Salome* and *Rosenkavalier* but also Otto Klemperer's innovatory work at the Berlin Krolloper, all of which he dismissed as 'cultural Bolshevism'. He introduced his 1924 season with the manifesto, 'Bayreuth is not there for any sort of hyper-modern vogues. This would contradict the style of works which after all were not written and composed as cubist, expressionist, or dadaist.' But signs of life did begin to appear shortly before he died, a mere four months after his mother. In that year, 1930, he mounted a *Tannhäuser*, conducted by Toscanini, which could no longer be described as 'marvellously unmodern' and which, despite the predictable difficulties created by the Wahnfried ideologues, began to take advantage of such triumphs of the modern stage as solid scenery (i.e. not painted flats) and creative lighting (not just illumination). By the time he died, Siegfried had achieved at least a measure of artistic independence for Bayreuth from the Fafner fraternity, and the idea of the festival as a national 'German holiday' was very much in abeyance.

Siegfried's widow Winifred maintained the new artistic impulse by bringing in up-to-date Berliners like Furtwängler and Heinz Tietjen, and from Munich the designer Emil Preetorius. The new team attempted no revaluation of Wagner's works, though Hans Mayer considers that there was some gain in the psychology of characterization, and there exist many reliable accounts of the superlative musical standards attained by singers like Frida Leider. But, schooled as Winifred was in 'defiant German fanaticism and wilful anachronism', it was not long before her old friend Adolf Hitler bailed Bayreuth out of pressing financial difficulties and helped turn the idea of a nationalist festival into reality, thus casting so damaging a spell upon Bayreuth that it has never since been entirely able to throw it off.

When the festival eventually reopened in 1951, the way at last seemed clear for the grandsons Wieland and Wolfgang to lay aside the old ideologies. Not only did the Wagner brothers get the dramatic strategy right – one of ceaseless revaluation – but they themselves showed how the vitality of the Wagnerian oeuvre was best demonstrated by productions that were works of art in their own right, and in Wieland's case often of genius. The problem which their success has brought out into the open is that of how the producer's inventiveness can coexist with the fixedness of Wagner's words and music.

Recourse was had to the professors, among them Ernst Bloch (Wieland resurrected his essay from the 1920s, 'Paradoxes and the Pastorale in Wagner' – even persuading him to rewrite it for the instruction of the Bayreuth audience), and Theodor W. Adorno, who advised that 'If Wagner's work is indeed truly ambivalent and flawed, then do him justice by developing only one kind of praxis for production, which accounts for the flaws and realizes them instead of covering them up'.

While Wieland was glad to invoke the professors, it remains unclear how far their ideas influenced his art. But he must at least have welcomed their *Naturphilosophie* and Hegelian dialectics as a smoke-screen to choke off resurgence of the old Bayreuth ideology. Wieland sought in each of his grandfather's works an underlying pattern which would satisfy his need to discover a classical unity behind the polymorphic romantic exuberance. He cut a path through the undergrowth of the composer's staging instructions to whatever he particularly wanted to see. This was generally far more successful with tightly integrated works like *Tristan* and *Parsifal* than it was with that untidy epic, the *Ring*. Wieland's style was a far cry from Wagner's own passionately detailed staging ideal, but it was a brilliant solution to those contradictions and inconsistencies that undermine the very notion of music-drama. If it refused to echo the more mimetic musical effects, it magnificently served the more abstract, Schopenhauerian, qualities of Wagner's scores. In the dim light, the mysteries of *Urwelt* and archetype were invited to declare themselves.

Radically critical of Wagner's intentions though this theatre of Wieland's was, it was one that assumed that the spectator sought identification and involvement with Wagner's mythology, however transformed (there were exceptions, though, as in the severe 1956 *Meistersinger* which hinted at qualities less than wholly admirable in Hans Sachs). But that was something that could no longer be taken for granted. It was a short step from dehumanized abstraction, designed to appeal to the spectator's unconscious, to productions that rejected the validation of contradiction as myth and insisted on the explication of mystery. Such was the programme of Walter Felsenstein's Komische Oper in East Berlin, which had evolved its art of *realistisches Musiktheater*. Felsenstein himself produced Offenbach, Mozart, Weber and Verdi but always managed to avoid Wagner, and when a toe was put in the ocean with *Der fliegende Holländer*, the staging was delegated to an assistant.

The plunge proper was taken by Felsenstein's pupil Götz Friedrich with the 1972 Bayreuth *Tannhäuser*. Nothing was left to the imagination, everything was on show. No sooner had the overture begun than Tannhäuser unexpectedly ran on stage to mime his rebellion against the Landgraf's college of minstrels and his defection to erotic fatigues at the court of Frau Venus. The Landgraf himself was subsequently shown as a fascist despot who rode to the hunt in a sedan chair, his household riddled with armed secret police. The deaths of Elizabeth and Tannhäuser heralded no redemption for the minstrel, but for the working men and women who thronged the stage at the final tableau. Thus the arrival in the Festspielhaus' 'teure Halle' of the arch heresy of alienation.

Friedrich's *Tannhäuser* was an outstanding production, at once both far more radical and more self-assured than the technological narcissism of his 1976 Covent Garden *Ring*. Faithful to Felsenstein's ideals, it refused to take Wagner exclusively on the terms of his own time and built no rainbow but a solid bridge between his world and our own. The Bayreuth old guard were shocked by a production that took away identification with an ideational conflict offering the good burgher the illusion that he actually knew something about Venus and the Virgin. Friedrich substituted a view of the opera that renewed Wagner's own critique of received notions about the individual and society instead of negating it through ritual presentation.

No wonder that that audience, for it was surely they, should have been scandalized by Patrice Chéreau, who couldn't even take Wagner's mythology sufficiently seriously to be interested in its explication on any level. 'What is a God?' he asked the students of the Bayreuth International Youth Festival, 'You tell me – I've never met one.' In its centenary the tetralogy was to be presented as an allegory of the nineteenth century: 'As a man of the theatre, I find it impossible to have costumes and scenery without relating them specifically to a particular time.' Thus his *Ring* began not with the Beginning or any such romantic conceit, but with Wotan and family as the aristocracy of 1848 with Bakunin and Co piling logs around them, while down on the Rhine its daughters toted for custom in a froth of crimson petticoats. This particular cultural bridge ended right in the centenary audience, with Gunther and Siegfried in dinner-jackets, Brünnhilde in a white evening gown. Hagen's vassals were of course armed with machine-guns. Instead of a funeral march for Siegfried (the true end of the *Ring*, says Hans Mayer elsewhere), everyone just trooped onto the stage to stare at the corpse, while at the very end the shape of things to come was not entrusted to the 'redemption through love' motif, but handed straight out to the audience. The men, women and children who have witnessed the devastation of the Gibichung palace (a Hollywood mansion, or perhaps the villa of an arms millionaire) and watched the gods (?) roast in Valhalla, line up at the front of the stage. They look down first into the orchestra, from which emerges only *that* theme – indeed no solution at all. So they gradually lift their eyes expectantly to the audience – from whom comes no intuition of hope but a raucous volley of boos and whistles.

After *Mahagonny* Brecht was convinced that a theatre of alienation was the true counterpart to the music-drama. It is doubtful that he could have foreseen any possibility of rapprochement between Wagner's world and his own, such as one actually does see attempted by Götz Friedrich. Chéreau's approach, while no less iconoclastic, is curiously detached, a fulfilment of Boulez's suggestion that it would be nice to see the *Ring* produced by someone who had stumbled on it more or less by accident, as indeed Chéreau had. Ingmar Bergman and Peter Stein had successively dropped out, Chéreau being hastily summoned to fill the gap.[1] In fact he had seen the *Ring* once before (in 1975), in Wolfgang Wagner's pedestrian production of 1970. Now at last Adorno could find his prescription adopted with wholehearted commitment. Chéreau made no bones that the only unity he could discern in the *Ring* was its contradictions, certainly one way of bidding farewell to dialectics.

With that settled it needed no apology for Chéreau to build a hydro-electric dam on the Rhine, set up steam-engines in the woods, hang an infuriating Fourier pendulum in Valhalla, stage the Valkyrie ride in a country churchyard, house Fafner in a garage, and so on and so forth, with each scene being staged for instant, show-stopping effectiveness (literally so, on account of vociferous audience reaction), rather than as parts in an evolving whole. Wagner himself was in retreat from the Industrial Revolution; what better jest than to call his mountain landscapes to order with Satanic mills. Nietzsche castigated Wagner for exactly this style of theatricality, contemptuously referring in *Der Fall Wagner* to 'a series of strong scenes, each stronger than the other – and much sage stupidity in between'.

---

1. It was apparently Boulez's sister who had suggested Chéreau.

Much of the importance of Hans Mayer's study, its special perspective, is because he has himself been in the thick of New Bayreuth and subsequent developments. He knew Wieland Wagner well and himself lectured and wrote in advocacy of his work. Götz Friedrich is both a close friend and a sometime pupil. Friedrich's evaluation of the *Ring*, the proletarian sympathy manifest in his productions, owes much to Mayer's socialist-humanist stance (it would be misleading to confine the breadth of his concern within the Marxist boundary). It is characteristic that Hans Mayer should refer to Wotan's dealings with Brünnhilde in *Die Walküre* as a 'bourgeois tragedy' with obligatory 'erotic connection'. He never loses sight of the irony of the profoundly undemocratic fact of Bayreuth when measured against Wagner's music-drama-for-all manifesto. Had the first volume of the Cosima diaries been available at his time of writing, he would no doubt have quoted the reported remarks of two peasant girls while the Festspielhaus was under construction: 'Very fine, but when it's finished *we*'ll never be able to get in!' (6 June 1873).

At times Professor Mayer all but anticipates Chéreau. He refers to the obstacles facing the producer who would 'make the course of action independent of the illusion-seeking instructions which the great Wagner, a theatre man of the nineteenth century, provided'. For, he continues, 'One can immediately see the fragility of the structures, the cracks in the design. From the standpoint of the contemporary dramaturg and director, the entire work is in many places simply too well made.' That remark offers no comfort to the intrepid director, who is further advised that after Wieland's abolition of the Teutonic *Ring*, it has become 'just as impossible now to portray the tetralogy as a myth … unless it can be understood why these glorious gods … must finally meet their end'.

Professor Mayer also develops a Rousseauesque ecological angle which was much in evidence in Chéreau's staging, with its caged woodbird and dried-up bed of the polluted Rhine (in *Götterdämmerung*). For the class struggle (proletarian's eye-view), of course, a producer need look no further than Shaw's *Perfect Wagnerite* of 1898. To Chéreau, whatever else one may think of the partly baked features of his show, at least belongs credit for having staged the celebrated Shavian analysis.

But although Professor Mayer's ideas have something in common with Chéreau's practice, where the French director's manifesto touches Mayer's line of thought it sounds wilfully naive. Though perhaps not ignorant ('I esteem Wagner's great dramaturgical gift in the relationship between the text and the music'), in practice at any rate Chéreau was negligent of that crucial interdependence of Wagner's words and music which Hans Mayer rightly recognizes as the most important single problem in staging music-drama.

Nietzsche praised Baudelaire as 'the first intelligent adherent of Wagner anywhere'. We can now greet Chéreau as Wagner's first intelligent detractor among practical men of the theatre – the first to sting Wagner for his vaunted 'theatricality', not as Nietzsche did with words, but with deeds. For Chéreau uses theatrical shock tactics not to compel the spectator to share an illusory world, but rather to show him why he should recoil from it. Wagner wanted to compel belief in his myth: Chéreau is plainly amused by the propagation of disbelief. And 'no belief' is certainly a much more comfortable standpoint than the incipient indifference of 'partial' belief. To have nudged Wagner over into the Brechtian camp is a *tour de passe-passe*, for the achievement is itself no more than a conjuror's *coup*. Still, at least as Hans Mayer says, 'one no longer goes to Bayreuth as if one were trying to find the way to the Grail'. If one has managed for some reason to get there on one's feet rather than one's *genoux* yet, like Nietzsche a hundred years ago, be unable to suppress a 'shudder at the prospect of these long cultural evenings', then one can always emulate the philosopher's flight from tetralogical tyranny to the Bohemian Woods, there to begin work on one's own *Menschliches, Allzumenschliches: ein Buch für freie Geister* (Human, All-Too-Human: a Book for Free Minds).

* * *

I was later to write much more positively about the Boulez/Chéreau *Ring* in my *Wagner and the Art of the Theatre* (2006), and indeed in 2018 to recommend it on BBC Radio 3 as the best DVD of the *Ring* then available. If I changed my mind about Chéreau it was through closer acquaintance and the improvements that were made. In 1976 'Brünnhilde's rock' in Act 3 of *Die Walküre* had been an uncomfortable mini-Matterhorn and in subsequent years was changed to a ruined chapel that seemed a late-echo of Arnold Böcklin's 'Isle of the Dead'. Wagner himself had actually approached Böcklin as prospective designer for the 1876 premiere and later also for *Parsifal*, but the artist turned him down. See also 'Reinventing Wagner after Hitler', Chapter 6 in this book.

Illustration 1: The Bayreuth Festspielhaus lit up for the Führer's birthday, 20 April 1939.

Chapter Six

Reinventing Wagner after Hitler[1]

The rehabilitation strategies of Wieland Wagner, Joachim Herz, Patrice Chéreau and Hans Jürgen Syberberg

It is, I think, not difficult to argue that those stage productions of Wagner's operas in the critical post-war period from 1951 until 1982 which are now rightly regarded as historically important, have been shaped by their response to the appropriations of Wagner by Hitler and the Nazis. I would like to consider a few significant examples. Ways had to be found for exorcizing the terrible ghosts; to cleanse the inheritance, in so far as this was possible, to reclaim Wagner, and to build bridges between the concerns of our modern world and those of Wagner in his own time. These are still the driving forces behind many of the best productions of the past 30 years.

---

1. Source: Lecture given in London and Milan, September 2016, published in: '*Mettere in scena Wagner. Opera e regia tra Ottocento e contemporaneità*' (Lucca: Libreria Musicale Italiana, 2019), pp. 127-36.

After the war, in the still-divided Germany, there were two principal strategies. In West Germany, productions were dominated by Wieland Wagner's quest to 'de-politicize' the operas. He did this by concentrating on their psychology. They were not about power and its abuse among Nordic and Germanic heroes. They were simply metaphors for the human psyche. Abstract settings would refute history, darkened stages would invite heightened concentration on the music. In East Germany, then under the thumb of Marxist socialism, the operas were 're-politicized'. Wagner the revolutionary of 1849 was resurrected, the *Ring* presented as an allegory of the evils of nineteenth-century capitalism. This interpretative angle carries forward to some extent into Patrice Chéreau's famous centenary staging of the *Ring*.[2] By 1976, ten years after Wieland Wagner's death, his brother Wolfgang's Bayreuth was more than ready to find a new direction. Sensationally it did so by calling in the French team of Pierre Boulez, Patrice Chéreau and Richard Peduzzi. This wasn't perhaps as 'political' a production as has sometimes been suggested. What it did do was to connect Wagner's ideas of theatricality with those of the modern world. In *Rheingold*, we begin with gods in baroque costumes. In *Götterdämmerung*, we end with Hagen in a scruffy lounge suit and Siegfried and Gunther in dinner-jackets. It was a liberation from all previous constraints, from the idea that the *Ring* was a coherent, synchronous drama. The path from 'fidélité', from 'Werktreue', to post-modern interpretation lay ahead.

An important dissenting voice was that of the East-German film-maker Hans-Jürgen Syberberg. He recoiled from what he considered, sometimes accurately and sometimes not, the 'escapist' strategies of most post-war productions. He argued that these wallowed quite culpably in guilt, egged on by leftist philosophers. What, in Syberberg's view, these stage productions had not done was to 'mourn' for that guilt by facing up to it. That was what he tried to do in his remarkable 1982 film version of *Parsifal*.[3] This grappled directly with Wagner's own awkward personality. It also grappled fearlessly with the history of Germany's problematic entanglement with this opera in particular and with Wagner as a whole. In Syberberg's film, psychology, politics, history and theatricality are all potently intertwined. Its legacy has impacted powerfully on the course of subsequent Wagner stage performance.

* * *

Let us now consider these 'reinventions' in greater detail. But first, I would like to emphasize just how seriously Wagner took the stage presentations of his operas. There were conductors he could entrust with the music, but there was no one but himself who could invent and execute the stage presentation. In a famous drawing by Adolph Menzel, he is on stage at Bayreuth in 1875 rehearsing the second act of *Siegfried*.

Stage direction was so important a part of his mission that his 15-year-old daughter Isolde's choice of a single, representative image for 1875 was her version of Menzel's

---

2. For my first impressions of the production, see 'Damming the Rhine', Chapter 5 in this book.
3. Richard Wagner, *Parsifal*, a film by Hans-Jürgen Syberberg, 2 DVDs, 1982 (www .filmgalerie451.de).

Illustration 3: Isolde Wagner's watercolour depiction of her father rehearsing on the Bayreuth stage.

Illustration 2: Wagner generally chose to be the stage-director rather than the conductor of his operas. Adolph Menzel's sketch shows him rehearsing Act Two of *Siegfried* on the Bayreuth stage in 1975.

drawing, to which she very observantly added the curving front shell of the 'invisible' orchestra.

The image is from Isolde's delightful pictorial biography of her father which she presented to him on his sixty-seventh birthday, 22 May 1880. It contains 65 watercolour paintings illustrating Wagner's life from 1813 to 1880.[4] The problems – and indeed the possibilities – of staging Wagner's works are of course immense. Wagner himself remained unsatisfied by what he'd achieved at Bayreuth in 1876. Since then countless directors have taken up the challenge and the history of their productions has become familiar.[5]

New Bayreuth cleanses the stable

We may now take up the story from 1951 when Wagner's grandsons, Wieland and Wolfgang Wagner, reopened the Bayreuth Festival. Their principal problem was the political one of distancing Bayreuth from its Nazification in the 1930s, something to which both brothers had been party. The solution? To create productions that gave every appearance of being apolitical, and to make a crazy attempt in and around the auditorium to censor people's conversations. 'Hier gilt's der Kunst!' (Art is what matters here), declared a poster displayed during the 1951 Bayreuth Festival, 'In the interest of

---

4. Dagny. R. Beidler, *Für Richard Wagner! Die 'Rosenstöcke-Bilder' seiner Tochter Isolde* (Cologne/Weimar/Vienna: Böhlau, 2013).
5. Major studies include: Dietrich Mack, *Der Bayreuther Inszenierungstil 1876-1976* (Munich: Prestel, 1976); Geoffrey Skelton, *Wagner at Bayreuth*, 2nd edition (London: White Lion, 1976); Oswald Georg Bauer, *Richard Wagner: The Stage Designs and Productions from the Premières to the Present*, trans. Stewart Spencer (New York: Rizzoli, 1983); Frederic Spotts, *Bayreuth: A History of the Wagner Festival* (New Haven and London: Yale University Press, 1994); Patrick Carnegy, *Wagner and the Art of the Theatre* (New Haven and London: Yale University Press, 2006); and Oswald Georg Bauer, *Die Geschichte der Bayreuther Festspiele*, 2 vols. (Berlin: Deutscher Kunstverlag, 2016).

Im Interesse einer reibungslosen Durchfüh-
rung der Festspiele bitten wir von Gesprächen
und Debatten politischer Art auf dem Fest-
spielhügel freundlichst absehen zu wollen.

„Hier gilt's der Kunst"

Die Festspielleitung
gez. WIELAND WAGNER   gez. WOLFGANG WAGNER

Bayreuth, im Sommer 1951

Illustration 4: 'Hier gilt's der Kunst!' (Art is what matters
here). Poster displayed during the first Bayreuth Festival
since the 1939-45 war and signed by Wieland
and Wolfgang Wagner.

the smooth conduct of the festival we kindly request that discussions and debates of a political nature should be avoided.'

'Hier gilt's der Kunst' was a revival of the same slogan, culled from *Die Meistersinger*, that their father, Siegfried Wagner, had invoked in 1925 to curb the singing of 'Deutschland über Alles', which during the previous year had been lustily sung by the audience after each performance of that opera. Wieland's *Meistersinger* of 1956 became known as 'Die Meistersinger ohne Nürnberg'. For Act Two, every trace of a timber-framed, folkloristic Nuremberg had been eliminated. The action took place simply on an open promontory. In irritated response to the outcry, Wieland softened his beautiful vision for the revivals from 1957 with skeletal outlines of Nuremberg houses, lattice-work fencing and an elderflower tree firmly planted in the ground.

Illustration 5: Otto Wiener as Sachs and Karl Schmitt-Walter as Beckmesser in
Act Two of Wieland Wagner's *Meistersinger*, 1957.

Wieland Wagner found his new direction by resurrecting the radical ideas and 1890s designs of Swiss artist Adolphe Appia. Appia had visited Bayreuth in 1882. He hated the cinematic, every-leaf-on-every-tree literalism of the scenery which, he felt, betrayed the transcendent luminosity of the music. He went away and prepared designs for the *Ring* that were inspired directly by the music and not by Wagner's scenic instructions. The designs showed only the symbolic essentials of each scene, the simplest of forms, his idea being that the dramatic ambience, the mood, the atmosphere would be created by stage lighting,

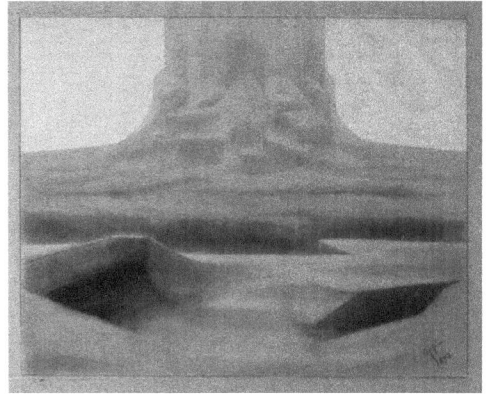

Illustration 6: 'Open space on a mountain top near the Rhine': Adolphe Appia's sketch for *Das Rheingold*, scene 2, 1892.

especially by the variability of electric lighting, which had begun to replace the inflexible gas lighting.

Appia's friend Houston Stewart Chamberlain urged Cosima Wagner to adopt Appia's designs for the 1896 *Ring*, the work at last returning to the Bayreuth stage for the first time since its first performance there in 1876. But Cosima scornfully dismissed the idea, saying that Appia's designs reminded her only of the pictures that the explorer Nansen had recently brought back from his North Pole expedition (1893-96). Besides, Herr Appia did not seem to realize that Wagner had himself staged the *Ring* in 1876 and that therefore there was 'no further scope for invention'.[6]

Way ahead of their time, Appia's futuristic ideas on non-representational staging were disseminated principally through his writings, not through their demonstration in actual stage productions.[7] There were to be notable exceptions, as when Toscanini invited Appia to design *Tristan und Isolde* (1923) for La Scala, and Oskar Wälterlin invited him to design *Das Rheingold* (1924) and *Die Walküre* (1925) for Basel. The plan had been for a complete *Ring* in Basel, but this foundered on the inadequacy of the stage technology and the vehement opposition of the local press. Let us remind ourselves of the romantic naturalism that was the aim – however imperfectly achieved in practice – of Wagner's own Bayreuth staging of the *Ring* in 1876.

Compare this with the stunning Appian simplicity of Wieland Wagner's staging of the same scene at Bayreuth in 1954. What unfortunately cannot be illustrated is how the red glow of the lighting (Brünnhilde's fire-girt rock) gradually changed to a blue

---

6. Cosima Wagner, letter to Houston Stewart Chamberlain, 13 May 1896, in Cosima Wagner, *Das zweite Leben*, ed. D. Mack (Munich: Piper, 1980), pp. 412-15. Cited in Edmund Stadler, *Adolphe Appia*, exhibition catalogue (London: HMSO, 1970), p. 12.

7. Adolphe Appia's first important publication is *Die Musik und die Inszenierung* (Munich: Bruckmann, 1899). English translation by Robert W. Corrigan and Mary Douglas Dirks, ed. Barnard Hewitt, as *Music and the Art of the Theatre* (Coral Gables, Florida: University of Miami Press, 1960). The standard edition is *Oeuvres complètes*, ed. Marie L. Bablet-Hahn, 4 vols. (Bonstetten, Switzerland: L'Age d'Homme, 1983-91).

Illustration 7: Siegfried's awakening of Brünnhilde: Josef Hoffmann's oil-sketch for scene 3 in Act Three of *Siegfried*. The artist's designs for the *Ring* are discussed in Chapter 3, p. 44.

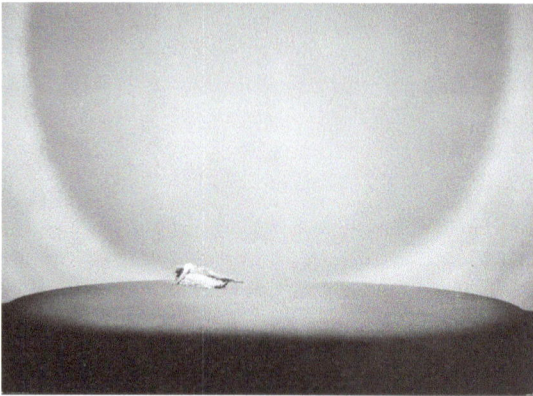

Illustration 8: Wieland Wagner's minimalist vision of the same scene as in Illustration 7, photographed in 1954.

firmament that seemingly heralded the dawn of a new world.

And let us now compare Appia's idea for the rocky gorge of the second Act of *Die Walküre* with Wieland's realization of the same scene. Here we see not a scene from Nature but a narrow prison, symbol of Wotan's entrapment. The ambience is that of Greek tragedy, not of a Germanic saga.

Wieland Wagner invokes Jung's 'archetypal' images, often reminiscent of the sculptures of Henry Moore. He invites us to experience Wagner not as an animator of gods, heroes and villains, but as a depth psychologist *avant le jour*. In his 1965 *Rheingold*, the piled-up hoard, supposedly concealing Freia, revealed a primitive female form that was an unmistakable image of sexuality and fecundity.

And in the second act of *Götterdämmerung* from the same 1965 *Ring*, it was archetypal totems that represented the household gods of the Gibichung Hall.

Illustration 9: 'A gorge stretches up from below to a high ridge of rocks.' Act Two of *Die Walküre*, as imagined by Appia in the 1890s.

Illustration 10: Wieland Wagner's vision of the same scene, 1952, with Hans Hotter as Wotan and Martha Mödl as Brünnhilde.

Illustration 11: A totemic golden ransom for Freia in scene 4 of Wieland Wagner's *Rheingold*, 1965.

Illustration 12: Archetypal sacred images preside over Act Two of *Götterdämmerung* in Wieland Wagner's production of 1965.

Wieland reaffirmed Wagner's own goal of opera as timeless myth, liberated from all specific historical reference. In purpose and effect this was a bid to de-politicize Wagner.

East Germany resurrects Wagner the political revolutionary

But on the Eastern side of the then 'Iron Curtain' that divided Germany, the opposite happened. Wagner was re-politicized. Here, not capitalism but Marxist cultural politics held sway. And it rediscovered the Wagner of 1849, the angry revolutionary who had stood at the barricades in Dresden and begun to conceive the *Ring*. The perfect blueprint lay to hand in George Bernard Shaw's *Perfect Wagnerite* (1898) – widely read in translation – which had unmasked the *Ring* as a metaphor for the evils of nineteenth-century capitalism. No production strategy could have been better suited to the prevailing, and strictly policed, ideology. And so this became the inspiration for

Illustration 13: Alberich as a factory boss, and Mime and the Nibelungen as proletarian slaves: designs by Rudolf Heinrich for Joachim Herz's Leipzig *Ring*, 1973-6.

Illustration 14: Wotan (András Faragó) and Fricka (Renate Härtel) as wealthy capitalists in Act Two of Herz's *Die Walküre* in Leipzig, 1973-6.

Illustration 15: Gunther Gibich's industrial power station: Rudolf Heinrich's setting for Act Two of *Götterdämmerung* in Herz's production in Leipzig, 1973-6.

Joachim Herz's important staging of the *Ring* in Leipzig, 1973-76, as you can see from the costumes and designs.

The Communist Party commissars wanted Herz to stage a Utopian ending to the *Ring*, but the vigorously independent-minded Herz stood up to them. The 90 men and women of the chorus crowded onto the stage to witness the destruction of Valhalla and the Rhinedaughters swooping down in gondolas to reclaim the *Ring*. At the end, in a cold, grey light, came a *tabula rasa* which neither affirmed nor denied the note of hope sounded in the music. Herz had reaffirmed the *Ring* as an explanatory myth of the industrial, capitalist nineteenth century.

The French route to the future: a bridge between Wagner's nineteenth century and the modern world

We must return to West Germany and to the Bayreuth of 1976. As I have said, ten years after Wieland Wagner's death his brother Wolfgang put an even greater distance between the unsavoury 1930s and 'New' Bayreuth by entrusting the centenary *Ring* production not, as every-one expected, to a German conductor, director and designer, but to the French team of Pierre Boulez, Patrice Chéreau and Richard Peduzzi. Chéreau is not known to have seen Herz's *Ring*, but plainly both Chéreau's and Herz's productions were variations on the Shavian interpretation of the work. Chéreau reforged the mythic construct of the *Ring* by building a bridge between Wagner's world – the industrial nineteenth century – and the concerns of the late twentieth century. Nature is no longer a paradise but, through man's greed for wealth, has become polluted,

Illustration 16: Siegfried's death at the dam across the Rhine in Patrice Chéreau's Bayreuth *Ring*, 1976, designed by Richard Peduzzi. The dam as it was seen in *Das Rheingold* is depicted in Chapter 5, p. 76.

Illustration 17: Wotan (Donald McIntyre) as a plutocratic geophysicist, with Hanna Schwarz as Fricka and Gwyneth Jones as Brünnhilde in Act Two of Chéreau's *Die Walküre*, Bayreuth, 1976.

Illustration 18: Gwyneth Jones's Brünnhilde, backed up by Karl Ridderbusch's Hagen, threatens Manfred Jung's Siegfried with the spear in Act Two of Chéreau's *Götterdämmerung*, Bayreuth, 1976.

its free-flowing rivers dammed to generate electricity.

Wotan has become a plutocratic geophysicist. In the cessation of the motion of the Foucault Pendulum in his laboratory he discerns 'das Ende', the extinction of planet Earth.

In Wieland Wagner's productions the acting had largely been stylized and restrained. Chéreau's characters are flesh-and-blood. The acting is impassioned. The drama is no longer symbolic but humanized – that of conflict between real people. Hagen's murder of Gunther has all the raw dramatic intensity of a Shakespearean tragedy.

Brünnhilde's immolation, in a setting indebted to Elia Kazan's famous crime-drama film *On the Waterfront* of 1954, is witnessed by ordinary working people and

Illustration 19: 'Fly home, you ravens!' Gwyneth Jones as Brünnhilde in her immolation in the final 'On the Waterfront' scene of Chéreau's *Ring*, Bayreuth 1976.

their children, representatives of what Chéreau described as 'a humanity which is enslaved and manipulated'.

'Parsifal' on the couch: Hans-Jürgen Syberberg's 1982 film

Let us conclude by considering the remarkable film version of *Parsifal* I mentioned earlier, whose 'reinvention' of Wagner is certainly more radical than the stage productions of Wieland Wagner, Joachim Herz or Patrice Chéreau. Hans-Jürgen Syberberg's *Parsifal* is both more extreme and more challenging, not least because the East-German film-maker was deeply critical of these and other stage directors whom he considered to be unduly influenced by influential Marxist philosophers like Adorno, Ernst Bloch and Herbert Marcuse. That charge is by no means proven against Wieland and Herz, and certainly not against Chéreau, but never mind.

The quixotic task that Syberberg set himself was to 'cleanse' *Parsifal*. He sought to rescue its romantic soul, and he believed this had to be done by completing what he maintained was Germany's necessary mourning (*Trauerarbeit*)[8] for its problematic, troublesome past. His *Parsifal* is the culmination of a series of previous films – including ones about King Ludwig and Karl May[9] – with which he had sought to exorcise the association between icons of German culture and their debasement by the Third Reich. Striking mercilessly to the core, he discovered in the unashamed Winifred Wagner, daughter-in-law to the composer and mother of Wieland and Wolfgang, an eloquent and honest witness to the past. He had little difficulty in persuading Winifred to talk on camera about her infatuation with Hitler and his role in the Bayreuth of the Thirties.[10] Here, at last, in 1975, Syberberg had found a key player who was prepared to give an unapologetic account of Bayreuth in the Third Reich.

But for Winifred's son, Wolfgang, who had striven since 1951 to keep the skeletons in the cupboard, this was what we'd now call a 'media' disaster of the first order. (Wieland had died all too prematurely in 1966.) Winifred's *Confessions* came out all over German television just as Wolfgang was preparing to consolidate Bayreuth as an international rather than a Germanic phenomenon. As we have seen, he had done this, quite scandalously to many of his countrymen, by inviting the French team of Pierre Boulez and Patrice Chéreau to stage the *Ring*, 'the' most quintessentially German work of all in 1976, its centennial year. In retrospect one can see that the scandal of the Winifred interviews only exacerbated the *furore* with which the Boulez/Chéreau *Ring* was initially greeted, but also that it played its own important part in winning a more open discussion of the Wagnerian problematic.

---

8. *Trauerarbeit*, literally 'work of mourning'. The concept first appears in Freud's 1915 essay 'Trauer und Melancholie', in which it is argued that the individual can overcome the loss of a loved person only by engaging in *Trauerarbeit*, that is, by undergoing a repeated, painful process of remembering and working through the grief.

9. *Karl May: Auf der Suche nach dem verlorenen Paradies*, 1974. *Ludwig: Requiem für einen jungfräulichen König*, 1972.

10. Hans-Jürgen Syberberg, *Winifred Wagner und die Geschichte des Hauses Wahnfried, 1914-1975*, 1975.

In the *Ludwig* film, and in a marathon, satirical and fantastical treatment of *Hitler: A Film from Germany*,[11] Syberberg had been mesmerized by Wagner's catastrophic hold over two very different kinds of romantic dreamer. But the result of his interviews with Winifred Wagner was to make Syberberg think that Wagner was more sinned against than sinning. He therefore sought to rescue him by making a film of *Parsifal*, the opera in which the composer most intimately confronts himself and his art. After the *Confessions of Winifred*, why not the *Confessions of Richard* in the shape of a version of his last opera?

Robert Lloyd, who plays Gurnemanz in the film, told me about how Syberberg viewed his conception.[12] Over breakfast one day – this was at Syberberg's house in Munich – Lloyd had plucked up his courage and asked the director how he perceived Wagner. Syberberg answered, 'Well, *Parsifal* is Wagner', to which Lloyd replied, 'You mean the character Parsifal?' 'No', retorted Syberberg, 'the opera is Wagner', and he went on to say that the opera was 'an autobiographical portrait of his musical and spiritual journey'.

* * *

In the film the sins and wounds of Klingsor, Kundry and Amfortas are identified with those of Wagner himself, and also of the Germany that gave rise to Hitler and would not take the proper steps to bury him. This then would be a film that rejected Wagner's pictorial scenario in favour of a psychological exploration of the opera, of its roots in Wagner's mind and of its historical afterlife. The opera would be reborn in the light of its relationship with its creator and with history. Thus it was that Syberberg conceived of locating all the events in, on or around a huge studio model of the composer's death mask, representing a physiognomic panorama of Wagner's soul.

The complete score of *Parsifal* was recorded before filming began. The conductor was Armin Jordan, with the Orchestre Philharmonique de Monte Carlo. With the exceptions of Aage Haagland as Klingsor and Robert Lloyd as Gurnemanz, the roles were played by actors who mimed to the pre-recorded voices of Wolfgang Schöne as Amfortas, Hans Tschammer as Titurel, Reiner Goldberg as Parsifal and Yvonne Minton as Kundry. Amfortas was actually acted by the conductor, Armin Jordan.

It is characteristic of Syberberg's imagery that the Amfortas-wound is treated as representative of a whole array of other wounds. Abstracted from Amfortas' body, his Wound is on public view as a suppurating pathological exhibit, carried about on a cushion by two female pages. The Wound is at once a symbol of a mortally ill monarchy, and an object of public shame. It is Germany's unassuaged shame and guilt, an object of fascination and horror until it can be healed. Because the opera is imagined as a psycho-drama where time has become space, Robert Lloyd's youthful, clean-shaven Gurnemanz doesn't visibly age between the first and third acts.

---

11. Hans-Jürgen Syberberg, *Hitler: Ein Film aus Deutschland*, 1977. The script and essays by Syberberg and Susan Sontag appear in Hans-Jürgen Syberberg, *Hitler: A Film from Germany*, trans. Joachim Neugroschel (Manchester: Carcanet New Press, 1982).

12. Conversation with Robert Lloyd at the conference 'Wagner's *Parsifal* and the Challenge to Psychoanalysis', Freud Museum (London), 3 July 2016.

Syberberg is not the first director to have been so mesmerized by Kundry that the opera becomes more the story of her redemption than that of Amfortas. She, brilliantly acted by Edith Clever (but, as has been said, sung by Yvonne Minton), and Amfortas are conceived of as the female and male halves of a single suffering self. They're bound together by her enforced seduction of him and the wounds thereby inflicted on them both. Both are Klingsor's victims. It is a pairing that balances that of the two Parsifals, for this is the film's most sensational novelty. There is a boy Parsifal, representing Jung's

Illustration 20: In the second act of Syberberg's film, Karin Krick's Parsifal II moves forward to supplant Michael Kutter's Parsifal I and to complete the therapeutic journey begun by him.

animus, and, yes, a female Parsifal, representing the anima. They're first seen together at the end of the prelude, when the camera closes in on the boy and girl Parsifals wrapped closely together in silent communion. Then the luxuriantly shock-headed boy gently breaks free and departs. He leaves his female counterpart behind to dream. Syberberg's idea is that while one Parsifal dreams the other enacts the dream – with the roles being reversed at the point of Kundry's kiss in Act Two. It's now the boy who dreams, while the action is taken over by the girl.

The pivotal moment comes when Kundry's kiss simultaneously awakens the boy's sexuality and overwhelming feelings of shame and guilt. Breaking free from her with the cry, 'Amfortas! Die Wunde!', his place is taken by the girl who has quietly stepped forward from a projection of the death mask. The boy briefly joins his voice with hers before he dissolves into soft focus and disappears.

It is the rather serious girl Parsifal who sets off on the long restitutional journey back to the Grail. And in Act Three, it is she, in her leather helmet and jerkin, who is rapturously received by Gurnemanz and Kundry in the Good Friday scene.

Syberberg handles this Good Friday scene with immense tenderness as Kundry and Parsifal look into each other's eyes. For the director this scene was of central significance in his project to cleanse and redeem Wagner from his sins and from those committed against him by the Third Reich. And indeed does this not chime precisely with Gurnemanz's 'Das dankt dann alle Kreatur, / Was all' da blüht und bald erstirbt, / Da die entsündigte Natur / Heut ihren Unschuldstag erworbt' (Thus all creation gives thanks for everything that blossoms and soon dies – absolved from sin, Nature today regains its innocence)? As the bells begin to toll, the figures advance towards the camera and disappear out of focus.

Illustration 21: With the return of the spear, Wagner's skull slowly splits apart, revealing the male and female Parsifals – Jung's animus and anima – reconciled, reunited and redeemed.

Back in the Hall of the Grail, Amfortas is already lying on his deathbed. The bleeding open Wound lies on a cushion alongside him in the foreground. Such is his agony that he cries out to the Knights to plunge their swords into him. And at this critical moment, the girl Parsifal appears, high up on the top of the skull, and holding a primitive crucifix. She's still but the harbinger of the missing spear: 'Nur eine Waffe taugt' (Only one weapon will serve), she sings. And then, below her and finding his way through the Knights, the boy Parsifal reappears with the sacred spear: 'Den heil'gen Speer, ich bring' ihn euch zurück!' (The holy spear, I bring it back to you). The girl joins him and they sing together of the healing of the Wound. Amfortas and Kundry are absolved from their sins and released to die beside each other. Both Parsifals now command 'Enthüllet den Gral, öffnet den Schrein' (Uncover the Grail, open the shrine), and the shrine that is Wagner's head, seen in profile, begins to split apart. Mists roll in to suggest it is now above the clouds. In its cleft appear together both Parsifals, who gently embrace. For Syberberg this is a resolution of the split consciousness seen in the two Parsifals – the animus and anima now healed and whole at last.

What are we to make of this extraordinary film? It's perhaps fair to begin by wondering whether the abundance of imagery in the film isn't excessive, even mischievously obscurantist. It's often hard not to feel as flummoxed as Parsifal when first confronted by the mysteries of the Grail ceremony. Hundreds of pages have been written in the attempt to explain and even justify the imagery.[1] But surely it shouldn't be necessary to read the footnotes to comprehend the film?

---

1. See Solveig Olsen, *Hans-Jürgen Syberberg and his Film of Wagner's 'Parsifal'* (New York/ Oxford: University Press of America, 2006), and the director's own book, Hans-Jürgen

I suspect that Syberberg himself would very likely retort that the very stuff of dreams is the irrationality of its imagery, let each one make of it what he may. There's no question that for Syberberg himself, the magician who has conjured it up, nothing is arbitrary and without significance – it's just that it can sometimes only be decoded with effort. And he could argue that the obscurities are a deliberate strategy to appeal to, to vex and agitate the viewer's own unconscious rather than to satisfy and flatter his rational response. We've seen how Syberberg considered his *Parsifal* to be the culmination of his own *Trauerarbeit*, his mourning for the evil that Germany leashed upon the world. Angered by what he sensed as the general lack of such therapeutic mourning in the East Germany all around him, and his knowledge of a similar lack in the West, Syberberg intended this film, like his earlier *Hitler: A Film from Germany* and his *Confessions of Winifred Wagner*, to question and challenge Germany's indifference. (The same endeavours are no less evident in, for example, the artworks of Anselm Kiefer and Joseph Beuys, the films of Werner Herzog, and in novels and plays by Thomas Bernhard, Peter Handke and Botho Strauss.)

But, and undoubtedly because he had hit the spot so precisely, the film had a frosty reception in both Germanies. He was accused, inter alia, of dallying with fascism, of being complicit with the very evil he seemed to be seeking to expiate. The wider cause of *Trauerarbeit* in both Germanies remained untouched by his *Parsifal*. It was only abroad, most noticeably in France, England and America, that the film was hailed as a telling analysis of Germany's problematic attitude to its past. Could it be speaking more eloquently about our fantasies around Germany than about the collective German psyche itself? Looking back on the film from the nearly 40 years that have elapsed since 1982, it's hard to imagine that it has in any way rescued the 'romantic soul' of the opera, a soul innocent of its subsequent history – a quest that simply isn't possible. But Syberberg has at least surely rescued *Parsifal* from the accusations of *mauvaise foi*, of anti-Semitism and advocacy of racial purity that have played too large a part in modern discussion of the opera. And he's done this while dealing honestly with the uses to which the work has been put, and not wallowing aggressively in retrospective guilt. The film's probing of Wagner's own psychology, of *Parsifal* as his valedictory self-analysis, has opened up perspectives that have left a rich legacy which has been fruitfully explored by subsequent stagings like that of Stefan Herheim at Bayreuth in 2008.

* * *

I hope my examples have illustrated not only the importance of the historical and social context in which Wagner is performed, is reimagined, but also how the context of post-war Germany has provoked new and very different interpretations. All of these 'reinventions' of Wagner may have been rooted in the need to exorcize the ghosts of Nazi appropriation, but it's in their discovery of new perspectives, or reinvigorations of old ones, that their true value lies: Wieland Wagner's emphasis on myth and his grandfather's indebtedness to Greek tragedy, Joachim Herz's assertion of Wagner the political

---

Syberberg, '*Parsifal*': *Ein Filmessay* (Munich: Wilhelm Heyne, 1982).

radical, of the *Ring* as about the evils of industrial capitalism, Patrice Chéreau's bridge between the world of the nineteenth century and the anxieties of modern times.

Syberberg's *Parsifal* is something of a special case in its unsparing analysis of Wagner's own psyche. In the end that analysis is not something that can ever be proved right or wrong. But it surely does have the resonance, the rich suggestiveness, of a great work of interpretative art.

Reinventing Wagner to assuage our own anxieties about him will never go away. He has, alas, become all too easy a target for those wishing to score cheap points at his expense. But the great directors I've tried to talk about have managed acute critical engagement with the problematic aspects of his works and their legacy, while also discovering new 'fidelities' to previously unsuspected aspects of Wagner's great, because inexhaustible, works.

Illustration 1: Neuschwanstein, photographed from the Marienbrücke by the author c.1962.

Chapter Seven

A Touch of Wagnermania[1]

One of the many challenges of location-filming is coming back with what you set out to capture. I had the good fortune to be one of the presenters of the documentary film on Wagner in BBC Two's 'Great Composers' series, first broadcast in 1997. It remains, to my entirely prejudiced mind, an engaging and exceptionally well-balanced introduction to Wagner's life and works. But viewers can have no idea of how close the programme came to being denied crucial footage of the Bayreuth Festspielhaus.

Permission for such filming had of course been obtained long before director Kriss Russman (subsequently making his mark as both composer and conductor) and his film crew set out. They had been filming first at Tribschen on Lake Lucerne and I joined them in the Bavarian Alps in May 1995 to tell the story of King Ludwig's part in Wagner's life before we went on to Bayreuth, the last and most important part of the trip.

After taking the train down from Munich, I was collected by Kriss from the tiny station at the end of the line and whisked off for supper. Returning to our quarters

---

1. Source: *Wagner News* (journal of The London Wagner Society), April 1998.

at Schwangau in the Schlosshotel Lisl und Jägerhaus, Ludwig's famous castles were suddenly there above us, floodlit and magical in the darkness. The turrets of Hohenschwangau, the relatively sedate castle where Ludwig spent much of his youth and later entertained Wagner, loomed up in front of the hotel. High in the pine forests half a mile away, was fairy-tale Neuschwanstein on its rocky eminence – Ludwig's ultimate dream of escape into the mists of courtly legend. The Schlosshotel was well in tune with the *genius loci*. In the bathrooms water sprouted from the beaks of gilded swans, while the birds were exquisitely embroidered into the bed linen. Doubtless the pillows were stuffed with their feathers.

I hadn't seen the castles for nearly 30 years but had never forgotten the breathtaking views of Neuschwanstein from the Marienbrücke, a hunter's bridge flung over a rocky gorge. It was from this spot that Ludwig had first seen the site for his lofty retreat, part liberation from his mother's company at Hohenschwangau, part homage to Wagner, and it was from there – on 22 May, Wagner's birthday – that, several hundred feet above the gorge's tumbling stream, we first filmed the castle.

Later, we humped the camera gear up interminable winding stairs into the Byzantine throne room, Ludwig's vision of the Hall of the Grail in *Parsifal*. Our cameraman Colin Waldeck, perilously perched in a Romanesque window embrasure, legs held in a safety embrace by an assistant, obtained bird's-eye shots of Hohenschwangau and the Alpsee far below. Kriss was already dreaming of a special-effects night sky with fireworks, an evocation of Ludwig's lakeside theatricals when Lohengrin's magical appearance had been enacted by a handsome aide-de-camp in a swan boat drawn slowly to shore.

Down in Hohenschwangau the castle guide, 'Poffi', was awaiting us. What he hadn't expected was to be asked to talk on camera about the Lohengrin-saga mural in the queen's apartments. There was consternation when he declared he'd left his lederhosen at home, and wouldn't perform without them. Eventually we persuaded him to settle, albeit uneasily, for a borrowed Bavarian jacket. While waiting to go on he chatted with me in the lobby, his jaws busy with chewing gum. Suddenly he was anxious again. Would it be OK for him to hang onto his *Kaugummi*? Unkindly, I thought perhaps not, and with this last talisman gone he bravely strode on for yet another assignation with the silvery knight.

Uncomfortably early the next morning (before the tourists arrived), we were shivering in the Venus grotto, hewn into the hillside behind Linderhof, the architectural homage of the 'Dream King' to the absolutist world of Louis XV. No use remembering that Ludwig had installed the very first electric generators in Bavaria in order to keep the grotto's pool at a steamy 20°C, power artificial waves and fire up pink and blue lighting effects. The idea was that I should address the camera, Lohengrin-style, from the little shell-coracle in which Ludwig had had himself rowed around the grotto. Mercifully the boat was decreed unsafe by the keepers of the cave. All too soon the excited cries of French schoolchildren were echoing through the air. Their nonchalant guide, having brutally summarized the story of Venus and Tannhäuser, wound up with a wave of her electronic baton, triggering a snatch of … Siegfried's Funeral March.

On that bright early summer day we were sorry to have to leave the still snow-capped peaks of Ludwig's Alpine landscape. After an unscheduled detour to catch glimpses of Schloss Berg and the Starnbergersee where the king had been found drowned in 1886, we arrived late at the hotel Bayerischer Hof in Bayreuth. Awaiting us were two faxes, one in German and a brisker one in English, regretting that a last-minute technical rehearsal prohibited filming in the Festspielhaus, nor would its director, the composer's grandson Wolfgang Wagner, who was in his late seventies, be available for interview. At the end of a long day this wasn't quite the welcome we'd been expecting. Kriss resolved to carry on as though the faxes had never arrived. At 8:15 next morning our entire team and equipment were encamped just inside the stage door.

I somehow persuaded the wary *Türmeister* to allow me the use of his phone to speak with Peter Emmerich, the press chief, whom I'd met on previous visits. Fifteen minutes later Kriss and I were shown up to Herr Emmerich's room on the first floor. We were quick to see he was caught between instructions from on high and his native disposition to be helpful. Kriss took the offensive, reminding him that camera crews cost money and that an appointment made months ago shouldn't have been so abruptly cancelled.

Emmerich asked whether we couldn't return to film at a more opportune moment? No, the budget would not stretch to a second visit. 'One moment,' said Herr Emmerich, 'I will speak to the technical director.' We held our breath. 'This way, please,' he smiled, putting the phone down and within minutes Colin and sound-recordist Terry Elms were setting up to film the huge stage and the secrets of the 'invisible' orchestra pit. The technical rehearsal, never in the least danger of being inconvenienced by the camera, consisted of trundling around some skeletal scenery for *Das Rheingold*. At the very least this would animate the otherwise empty stage.

Meanwhile I conversed with Peter Emmerich who was keeping a nervous eye on proceedings. Slowly I prised out the truth. A short while before, Channel 4 had screened a 'Wagnermania' series, with swastika banners and Wolfgang's own son, Gottfried, denouncing his family and Bayreuth as an unpurged hotbed of nationalism, anti-Semitism and worse, while driving around the Festspielhaus (from which he'd been banned). These programmes – presenting a totally unbalanced picture – had evidently only just become known in Bayreuth. Jumping to the conclusion that 'Wagnermania' had been a BBC disease (other British television channels not being on the Franconian radar), the management had wished to slam its doors against a further outbreak.

As I calmly defended the good name of the BBC, the relief in Emmerich's face was palpable. Our filming which had begun so tensely ended in happier mood. But there was still the matter of the interview with Wolfgang. He was very, very sorry but we really would have to come back for that. No, retorted Kriss, any return was out of the question – it was now or never. Surely Herr Wagner would not be pleased if this major documentary on his grandfather, to be shown around the world, were to fail to include his own authoritative account of everything achieved over the 30 years of his sole direction of the festival? Would he not talk for at least a few minutes with Mr Carnegy, who had interviewed him for *The Times* back in 1968? 'One moment, please,' and barely had Peter Emmerich disappeared than our quarry strode onto the stage in the most genial of moods. 'Herr Carnegy! Wie geht's Ihnen?' Introductions were swiftly made.

We had asked for minutes but were rewarded with a full half-hour in which Wolfgang not only described the achievements of 'Werkstatt Bayreuth' but skilfully defended himself against the calumnies of his son and the German press. Sadly, this footage for which we had all worked so hard fell, with much other good material, on the cutting-room floor. I only hope it was kept for the archives.

Part Three

A Quartet of Conductors

Illustration 1 : Arturo Toscanini at the height of his powers – blazing with authority and conviction but in private often racked with despair.

Chapter Eight

Toscanini: Champion of the Divine Art[1]

It is not unknown for artists to secrete lucky charms about their person before braving the public. But in the unrecorded history of these inspirational talismans there are unlikely to be discovered any as unsavoury as the handkerchief spotted with menstrual blood that was tucked into Toscanini's pocket as he took the podium on 14 November 1936, to conduct the Vienna Philharmonic in a programme that included Cherubini's Symphony in D Major and the Second Suite from Ravel's *Daphnis et Chloé*. The object in question had been solicited by the 69-year-old Toscanini from Ada, the 39-year-old wife of Enrico Mainardi, the most prominent Italian cellist of his generation. It was Ada who, of Toscanini's many lovers, was the one who appears to have excited him most and to have lasted longest in his transient and stormy affections. 'I received our Holy Shroud', he told her, 'just as I was going up the stairs in the Musikverein. I conducted the concert with it jealously hidden in my pocket, and it was a real inspiration. … For the love of God, Ada, it's you who bring me to such excess. Only you could exalt me to

---

1. Source: 'Champion of the Divine Art', *Times Literary Supplement*, 10 May 2002, pp. 22-23.

the point of dreaming up such fantasies. If only you had seen me at the moment when my eyes gazed upon that diaphanous veil, sprinkled with your blood!'

It is a tantalizing feature of Harvey Sachs' collection of Toscanini's letters[2] that while it tells us enough, and perhaps more than enough, about the great man's adoration of Ada, it remains largely silent about the lady herself and the spirit in which she went along with insistent demands that a few months later included a presumably non-horticultural request for 'the tiny flowers from Ada's little garden'. Sachs does not provide a photograph of Ada, nor indeed of anyone other than the maestro himself; nor is he helpful with clues about what other objects concealed about the conductor's person may have fuelled that fiercely commanding gaze.

The absence of anything other than the most basic information about Ada is remiss in that a substantial proportion of the 700 or so letters in the book is addressed to her. Toscanini had known Ada since at least 1917, but took up with her seriously only in what was for him and the rest of the world the crossroads year of 1933 when, in response to Hitler's accession, he pulled out of the Bayreuth Festival. He was at the height of his powers, throwing his international fame into the struggle against fascism. She was 30 years younger, a beautiful woman who, not so politically perturbed and possibly of anti-Semitic disposition, showed up in Bayreuth in 1937: 'You weren't obliged to go,' expostulated Toscanini. 'Who invited you? Furtwängler? You and your husband have stomachs of iron!' Their affair lasted until 1939, after which the maestro resumed where he had left off nearly 20 years before with a married Viennese lady, Elsa Kurzbauer: 'Sorceress!! I still love you, and I desire you even more intensely.'

Toscanini had been married since 1897 to Carla De Martini; it sounds as though it was a life sentence for them both. There is something curiously touching about the subterfuges to which he had to resort in the attempt to keep Carla in the dark about his serial philandering. But it seems that when she stumbled upon his love letters, she was more prone to bouts of irritation and agitation than to confrontation. And in the longer term – when passions had cooled – many of his mistresses became her friends. There was certainly plenty for them to grumble about together. We have to imagine Toscanini in July 1933 studying Bach's B Minor Mass and Beethoven's *Missa Solemnis* while hiding his letters-in-progress to Ada between the pages of the scores where, he tells her, 'they underwent went their purification!'. Incoming mail was no less problematic. He instructs her to 'change and vary how you address [the envelopes]. Use the typewriter sometimes, write by hand at other times.' There was fun to be had with pseudonyms, though Carla, not surprisingly, was undeceived by letters addressed to 'Antonio Trascuri' and 'Icinio Artù-Rostan' (these not from Ada but from a much earlier flame, the soprano Rosina Storchio, with whom he had had a son in 1903).

Toscanini eventually destroyed the greater part of Ada's letters and those sent by other lovers. He would have been horrified that his own have not merely survived but found their way through to an auction house and publication. In 1936, his advice was sought about the advisability of publishing new information about Verdi's love-life. 'These poor great men aren't left alone even when they're in their graves!' Toscanini told Ada. 'I have always adored Verdi as artist and man since my adolescence. Why should I get bogged down in such useless details of his life which bring him down to the level of other men? And if he liked women, what harm was there in that? He wrote *Falstaff* when he was eighty years old, *Otello* when he was seventy-four; do you think that a man of such a fibre would be satisfied with doing nothing but reciting the Ave Maria?' Nor, of course, was Toscanini, and he goes on to ask 'why stick one's nose into others' boudoirs? ... for pity's sake stop short of the bedroom threshold'.

With the publication of his own intimate letters, with their word-play on Ada's coital cries and allusions to precious nooks and crannies and so forth, the threshold of his own bedroom room has been breached irrevocably. In truth, though, his lover's prattle is not over-imaginative, and it is hard to imagine that its publication will have much, if any, effect on a reputation that will always rest with his legacy of recordings, artistic integrity and opposition to fascism, all of which are well documented. But if these letters reignite curiosity about his recordings and the central part he played in twentieth-century international musical life, so much the better. When Harvey Sachs published his life of Toscanini in 1978, only a handful of his letters had come to light. While it cannot be said that those now published add anything very significant to the story outside the bedroom door, it is obviously valuable to be able to catch glimpses of the cut-and-thrust of it in his own words. The letters to Ada are eloquent also of his wider concerns in the 1930s. The collection as a whole gives a fair conspectus of his life from 1885, when he was a 17-year-old student at the Royal School of Music in Parma, right through to 1956, the year before his death, just short of his ninetieth birthday.

On the podium he blazed with authority and conviction. But in private, Toscanini was often racked by despair that he was falling short of his ideals, and by despair for humanity in general. Over and over again he insists that he is an artist without vanity and that his only goal is to serve the music. Conducting the Brahms *Requiem*, *Die Meistersinger* and *Falstaff* at the Salzburg Festival in 1936, he complains that, 'When the orchestra comes back to me after having been with other conductors, it's in bits and pieces. I can tell you that the other evening, the hatred was flashing from my eyes against myself, against everyone. ... At the last performance of *Falstaff* that I conducted I even hated the music.' Admittedly there were also other things on his mind; Sachs speculates that he may have been struggling to fight off a pressing invitation to break his self-imposed exile and conduct again in his beloved homeland. But he held his course, eventually also withdrawing from Salzburg after the Anschluss.

We get a glimpse in 1937 of what he felt when things were going well in his conducting, in this case in the Adagio of Beethoven's Ninth:

> Do you know that at the modulation to E-flat I always conduct with my eyes closed? I see extremely bright lights far, far away; I see shadows moving around, penetrated by rays that make them even more disembodied; I see flowers of the most charming shapes and colours. And the very music I'm conducting seems to descend from up there – I don't know where![3]

---

3. Sachs, *Letters of Arturo Toscanini,* p. 298.

He was, of course, easily infuriated by other conductors, as by hearing Henry Wood and the BBC Symphony Orchestra in the same work: 'Shouldn't the Penal or Civil Code deal with crimes that are committed to the detriment of musical masterpieces? … The first movement was a funeral march. The scherzo played at 138 to the dotted half [Beethoven's metronome marking is 116] was completely off the rails! The adagio was adagissimo … and the Finale was so choppy that it made me angry.' So much for the founder of the Proms.

But when Toscanini arrived in London a week or so later to conduct the same orchestra (Beethoven's Ninth again and the Brahms *Requiem*) he was happy to report that it was 'very easy to rehearse with this orchestra. For me, it's superior to all others, at least for its magnificent discipline'. Not that this prevented a disastrous rehearsal: 'I stopped after three-quarters of an hour. That first movement of the Ninth always makes me despair.' It took 'a magnificent performance of Shakespeare's *Richard the Second*' with Gielgud to put his 'nerves back in order'. Although not cited by Toscanini, Richard's 'Ha, ha; keep time! How sour sweet music is / When time is broke and no proportion kept' could scarcely have fallen on a more receptive ear.

Back in New York, his bugbear and improbable associate was Leopold Stokowski, with whom he had to share the NBC Symphony Orchestra for a couple of seasons – one assumes that its management wanted to please all tastes. Stokowski tried to wrest the American radio premiere of Shostakovich's Seventh from Toscanini, who had to fend him off with a letter of exemplary restraint in (uncorrected) English:

> Don't you think, dear Stokowski, it would be very interesting for every body and yourself too, to hear the old Italian conductor (one of the first artist, who strenuously fought against fascism) to play this work of a young Russian antinazi composer? … May be I am not an intense interpreter of this kind of music but I am sure I can conduct it simply with love and honesty. Beside that this performance will have for me to-day a special meaning.[1]

Toscanini won out, his feelings about Stokowski being more accurately expressed in a letter drafted but never sent:

> This afternoon you have vitrolized Franck's Symphony … Never in my long life I have heard such a brutal, bestial, ignobil, unmusical performance like yours – not even from you. The Divine Art of Music too, has its own gangster like Hitler and Mussolini. … Believe me, you are ready for mad-house or for jail. … Hurry up!!![2]

Toscanini's dealings with the two fascist leaders themselves, whom he respectively dubbed 'the Madman, the Teutonic criminal' and 'the Great Delinquent from the Romagna', are well documented in the *Letters*. Back in 1919, strange to recall, Mussolini's manifesto had included abolition of the Italian monarchy, upper house of Parliament,

---

1. *Ibid*, p. 385.
2. *Ibid*, p. 382.

titles of nobility and compulsory military service. These were all causes dear to Toscanini's radical-libertarian ideals, and the conductor lent him his support, even going so far as to stand as a 'Fascist group' candidate in the elections of 16 November 1919. The electorate, however, were unimpressed and Mussolini swung quickly from the extreme Left to the extreme Right; Toscanini abandoned his political aspirations, but continued to use his formidable standing as a world musical figure to fight his corner.

In 1929 Mussolini sent a telegram congratulating Toscanini and his company on a triumphal visit to Vienna and Berlin. It did not fail to speak of La Scala's role in representing 'the new spirit of Contemporary Italy which unites to its will to power the necessary harmonious discipline required in every field of human activity'. Toscanini's measured response was intended to leave the *Duce* in no doubt about where his priorities lay: 'Today, as yesterday and always, I serve and will continue to serve my art with humility, but with intense love, certain that in so doing I am serving and honouring my country.' What he did not say was that he had just resigned his directorship of La Scala and had resolved to make his future with the New York Philharmonic. But he never ceased to be a thorn in Mussolini's side, or to defend prominent Italian musicians persecuted by the Fascists.

On his visit in 1899 to Bayreuth he had deplored 'the complete lack of good ensemble among orchestra, chorus and singers: the last, I can tell you just between us, are dogs. These Bayreuth performances are a real hoax for people like me who are hoping to hear perfection.' The immediate cause of his censure was Hans Richter, conductor of *Die Meistersinger*, and it is likely that Toscanini would also have heard *Parsifal* under Franz Fischer and the *Ring* under Siegfried Wagner. The latter, probably aware that standards were indeed some way short of 'perfection', in due course became a great fan of Toscanini's, and it was at Siegfried's invitation, in 1930, that the Italian became the first non-Teutonic maestro to conduct at Bayreuth. His performances of *Tannhäuser* and *Tristan* won over even Cosima's daughters, Daniela Thode, Blandine Gravina and Eva Chamberlain, who until then had been implacable defenders of Germanic hegemony in all things Wagnerian.

Toscanini spoke his mind. He informed Daniela that he could not 'agree with you regarding the lighting at the change from the Venusberg to the valley', and told Blandine, who had supported a proposal to make recordings, that 'it is impossible for me to take on so demanding and, above all, so unpleasant a job as that of making records!'. In a characteristically helpful note, Sachs points out that the latter refusal is understandable, in that Toscanini, whatever the quality of his interpretations, was dissatisfied with the playing of the Bayreuth orchestra. He was persuaded to return in 1931 (for *Tannhäuser* and *Parsifal*), when he was still complaining (to Carla) of the difficulty of getting singers and orchestra together for proper ensemble rehearsals.

It was to be his last appearance on the Green Hill. Although Toscanini was booked for the next (1933) festival, Hitler's accession to power inevitably led to his withdrawal. In March of that year, the maestro joined a group of largely Jewish colleagues active in America in sending Hitler a cable protesting against the dismissal of Jewish musicians from their posts. When Hitler responded with a message trying to sweet-talk the conductor into not abandoning the festival, Toscanini, bizarrely addressing the Führer in English, prepared the ground for his non-appearance:

it would be a bitter disappointment to me if any circumstances should interfere with my purpose to take part in the coming Festival Plays, and I hope that my strength, which the last weeks here taxed severely, will hold out.[3]

A month later, he is writing to tender his formal resignation from the festival, marking not only his final break with Bayreuth but with Germany as well. But he continued to treat the pro-Nazi Wagner family as respected friends, while at the same time making it clear that he wished 'the Pharisees' chased from 'the Temple together with the perjurer Richard Strauss' (who had taken over the performances of *Parsifal* he had hoped to conduct). Later, befriending Siegfried and Winifred's staunchly anti-Nazi daughter Friedelind, he told her that Bayreuth had been 'the deepest sorrow of my life'.

While Toscanini's resistance to fascism is adequately chronicled by his correspondence, it is disappointing that Sachs was not able to dig out more letters to his professional colleagues. It appears, for example, that nothing survives of his correspondence with Verdi's and Puccini's publisher, Giulio Ricordi, nor is there anything to the impresario Giulio Gatti-Casazza, with whom he worked so closely both at La Scala and at the Met. Let us hope that such letters may one day come to light; in the meantime the editor and publishers would have done better to have dropped the inclusive definite article from the title of this compelling volume.

---

3. *Ibid*, p. 138.

Illustration 1: 'When I'm into Wagner, I'm out with myself': Otto Klemperer at the Berlin Kroll Opera, 1929.

Chapter Nine

Klemperer: Sufferings and Greatness[1]

The colossus of London musical life in the 1960s was Otto Klemperer. A crippled giant of a man well into his seventies, face half paralyzed, he was helped to the platform, made his way haltingly to the rostrum, curtly acknowledged the applause, settled on to a high stool and unleashed performances of matchless spiritual conviction. It was known that he had been launched by Mahler's commendation; that he had championed Stravinsky, Schoenberg, Janáček, Hindemith and Weill in the 1920s; had left Nazi Germany for America; been musical director of the Budapest Opera after the war; and shuttled about a bit in relative obscurity until Walter Legge of EMI brought him to England to begin a long and fruitful association with the Philharmonia Orchestra. He had survived appalling illness and injury, the dislocations of exile, the affronts of

1. Source: 'The Irreproachable Daemon', *Times Literary Supplement*, vol. 1, 6 April 1984, p. 376, and 'Beethoven's Beethoven', *Times Literary Supplement*, vol. 2, 13 September 1996, pp. 13-14.

misunderstanding and neglect. His resurrection brought a sense of cultural continuity to a post-war musical world uncertain of its values.

Klemperer was a musician who did not waste words. As Peter Heyworth remarks at the outset of the first volume of his biography, its subject might have raised an ironic eyebrow at its length.[2] But in truth no aspect of this indefatigably researched and finely written book needs apology, least of all its length. For Klemperer's was a life that cannot properly be unfolded without a thorough understanding of its complex background. In supplying that, Heyworth makes a major contribution to the history of European musical life in the first 30 years of the century.

Meticulous in his research, Heyworth worked on it for years, completing all but the final half-chapter before his death in 1991. He left the task of completion in the capable hands of John Lucas, a former colleague on *The Observer* and the biographer of Reginald Goodall and Thomas Beecham. It is a long book; it was well worth the wait.

When the young Klemperer emerged from his musical studies he was regarded as a promising pianist, but from the moment in 1905 when he conducted the off-stage band for Mahler's Second Symphony in the composer's presence, his path was set. Mahler's personal recommendation, scrawled on a visiting card, secured him a junior conducting job at Angelo Neumann's German Theatre in Prague. It was a frustrating, operetta-ridden apprenticeship, from which he was rescued in 1910 when a second commendation from Mahler, this time in a telegram from New York, 'Klemperer zugreifen' ('Grab Klemperer') won him an assistant conductorship at Hamburg, his home town. He made his debut there with *Lohengrin* and electrified the critics. Two years later he was given two and a half weeks to prepare his first *Ring* cycle. It is no wonder that the pressures imposed by the repertory system nearly made him give up: at one point he wrote to a bookseller in Prague asking if he'd take him on.

Among the many testimonies from this period cited by Heyworth, none rings truer than that of Lotte Lehmann, whom Klemperer was coaching as Elsa:

> Klemperer sat at the piano like an evil spirit, thumping on it with long hands like a tiger's claws, and dragging my terrified voice into the vortex of his fanatical will. ... [Klemperer] belonged to the category of conductors who made one tremble, yet one was blissful when he was content. ... Toscanini made one do things because it hurt him if one didn't. Klemperer one obeyed with gritted teeth. ... He was always a terrible demon. ... one was hypnotized.[3]

From Hamburg he moved to Strasbourg in 1914 as deputy musical director under his old teacher Hans Pfitzner. Although he is now somewhat disregarded, Pfitzner was a central figure in his day, and Heyworth brings him sharply into focus. Pfitzner commanded Klemperer's respect not least because of his total identification with what he was conducting. When, during the second act of *Die Meistersinger*, it was evident

---

2. Peter Heyworth, *Otto Klemperer: His Life and Times*, vol. 1: 1885-1933, vol. 2: 1933-1973 (Cambridge: Cambridge University Press, 1983, 1996).

3. Heyworth, Klemperer 1, p. 74.

that the Beckmesser was too ill to continue, Pfitzner handed over the baton to an assistant, had himself shaved and made up, then went on stage to play the role in the final act. Pfitzner's passionate belief in *Werktreue* (fidelity to the work) exercised a lasting influence on Klemperer.

His first job as full musical director was at Cologne (1917-24), a post not wholly congenial to a man of his temperament and inclinations, for there 'opera was popular precisely because it so rarely provoked thought'. Fritz Rémond, the intendant, had no comprehension of *Werktreue*, believing that it was the producer's function to decorate the action with business. Klemperer did as much as anyone could have done to counter this attitude. He put on Busoni's *Turandot* and *Arlecchino*, and it was at least partly under his influence that he reacted against the 'upholstered orchestral textures' that had been typical of pre-First-World-War performances, including his own, and which were still the style of conductors like Bruno Walter, Erich Kleiber and Wilhelm Furtwängler. Klemperer saw the point of Busoni's anti-Wagnerian stance and his belief that *Junge Klassizität* (rejuvenated classicism) was the right path out of the late-romantic impasse. 'Wenn Wagner mir gefällt, gefalle ich mir nicht', he remarked in 1917 (when I'm into Wagner, I'm out with myself). After he left Cologne, at the age of 39, he never conducted the *Ring* again.

The world that dawned in 1918 was, Klemperer said, one 'in opposition to Wagner'. The immense changes that took place at the end of the war were closely mirrored in Klemperer's person and career, and are charted skilfully by Heyworth. Klemperer emerged with one foot in the late-romantic world of Mahler, Pfitzner, Schreker and Zemlinsky; and the other in the brave new worlds of Busoni, Janáček, Stravinsky, Krenek, Hindemith and Weill. After the war, music could no longer mean 'German music'.

In May 1922 he introduced *Petrushka* in a double bill with the first performance of Zemlinsky's *Der Zwerg*. Although, predictably enough, *Petrushka* was derided by the chauvinists as 'wry and dehumanized', 'a silly pantomime', 'the work of a Dadaist', and so on, Richard Strauss and a number of others were enthusiastic. This was the beginning for Klemperer of a long association with Stravinsky's music. It was an association that, strangely enough, did not include conducting *The Rite of Spring*, apparently because he protested that he couldn't beat its irregular metres.

In 1921 he chose an all-Schoenberg programme for his Berlin conducting debut, but he was soon in retreat from the expressionist aesthetic to which those works of Schoenberg that he admired belonged, and he made no secret of his dislike of the new dodecaphonic idiom. A month later he returned to Berlin for a performance of Mahler's Second Symphony that became a corner-stone of his reputation as a Mahlerian. 'Sobriety and ecstasy are the poles of his conducting', reported Walter Hirschberg: 'He has the ability to sink himself in a work so as to convey its innermost core, to place formidable competence and composure at the service of emotion, so that intellect and emotion become one'. Although his gestures on the podium were still extravagant, it was not only the New York critic Lawrence Gilman who observed (1924) that the histrionics were no longer the whole man but were a mask concealing disciplined sobriety, an almost puritanical severity:

He hovers over his orchestra like some fabulous, gigantic bird-man, menacing and inescapable. He growls audibly at his men, and once at yesterday's performance he almost roared. ... But these are external things. In Mr Klemperer's projection of the music we found nothing of the melodramatic, nothing of the sensational.[4]

There were triumphant visits not only to America but also to the Soviet Union. In Germany he was now in some danger of annoying both the powerful lobby of aggrieved Weimar conservatives (who found his interpretations over-analytical and intellectual), and supporters of Busoni's new classicism, who accused Klemperer of backsliding because he still performed the late-romantic masterpieces.

From Cologne Klemperer moved in 1924 to Wiesbaden, where he was to spend three of the happiest years of his life. But it was the call to Berlin for which he was waiting, and this came in 1926 when Leo Kestenberg, the principal figure behind the musical life of the young Weimar Republic, offered him the directorship of Berlin's second opera house: this was the recently reopened Staatsoper am Platz der Republik, adjacent to the Reichstag, and known as the Kroll Opera. Kestenberg's somewhat confused aim was that it should be both a wing of the *Volksbühne* (providing opera for a broad public) and a workshop for operatic renewal.

Klemperer's achievements at the Kroll are one of the most inspiriting chapters in the story of how opera at last shrugged off moribund nineteenth-century performing practice and became a living art. Repertory classics were given performances that repudiated the Wilhelminian ostentation almost universally aimed at in the old court theatres. Klemperer could now fulfil Mahler's old ambition of being not just the conductor but also 'the guiding stage-artist of the opera'. One of the greatest hits at the Kroll was a production of the original one-act version of *Der fliegende Holländer*. The work was drastically demythologized, the Dutchman being stripped of his beard and Senta's companions set not to spin but to make fishing nets. T.W. Adorno observed that the Kroll had 'mobilized a reserve of actuality in Wagner ... which will explode today or tomorrow' – as it did nearly 50 years later in Patrice Chéreau's Bayreuth production of the *Ring* in 1976.

The many modern works given at the Kroll included Hindemith's *Cardillac*, *Neues vom Tage* and *Hin und Zurück*; Stravinsky's *Oedipus Rex*, *Mavra*, *Petrushka* and *The Soldier's Tale*; five works by Krenek; Schoenberg's *Erwartung* and *Die glückliche Hand*; Weill's *Jasager*; Janáček's *From the House of the Dead*; and Debussy's *Jeux*. Klemperer took on nothing lightly (he rebutted attempts to pin a 'modernist' label on him) and projects sometimes floundered. He backed out of Weill's *Aufstieg und Fall der Stadt Mahagonny* (he took moral exception to the brothel scene), and out of Schoenberg's *Von Heute auf Morgen*. *Wozzeck* would have seemed a natural for the Kroll, but Klemperer never conducted it, nor was Berg's orchestral music ever played at the Kroll concerts.

All told, the repertoire was not the kind one would naturally associate with a theatre supposedly dedicated to the operatic education of the common man. The incongruity between Klemperer's aims and those of the Volksbühne was an instrumental factor

---

4. *Ibid*, p. 224.

leading to the Kroll's closure in 1931 (a disgraceful piece of cultural politic, expertly untangled by Heyworth). Kestenberg's faith in 'the oneness of socialism and music' was itself part of the problem. For if he didn't exactly believe that the *Volk* must love the highest *Bühne* when they saw it, he did believe that education would get them there in the end. But the middle-brow Kroll clientele had little interest in difficult modern works, wanting only *Carmen, Aïda* and the other staple fare of the wealthy bourgeoisie. The audience, said Klemperer, had expected 'big singers, big arias, big applause'.

Although Klemperer fought hard to save the Kroll, he found himself caught in a revolution that went beyond his own, primarily musical, aims. He clashed with his dramaturg, Hans Curjel, over the latter's choice of designers like Moholy-Nagy and Schlemmer. It was one thing that the stage should be purged of stage business and decoration, quite another that Bauhaus constructivism should take its place.

When the Kroll closed, Klemperer joined Leo Blech and Erich Kleiber as one of the three principal conductors at the Staatsoper Unter den Linden. But this was unsatisfactory from everyone's point of view, Klemperer regarding the repertory conditions there as inimical to the principles on which he had based his professional life. Meantime the Nazis were moving swiftly to power, though Klemperer seemed not to sense the danger. On 1 April 1933 he read Roger Sessions a prose-poem he had written in praise of the New Order in Germany. The next day he informed his Orthodox brother-in-law that the Jewish question was basically a religious one, suggesting that a Jewish palatine guard should be formed to protect Hitler. Assuming this was not a Klemperer *Witz*, Heyworth is surely right in hazarding that such notions were at least partly sparked by Klemperer's belief that the Weimar authorities had betrayed the Kroll. On 3 April he finally woke up and was persuaded to flee to Switzerland. There could have been no more ironic afterword to the Kroll experiment than that after the infamous Reichstag fire on 27 February 1933 its building was commandeered as the Reichstag's new home. Looking back years later, Klemperer felt that his subsequent career (first with the Los Angeles Philharmonic, then with the Budapest Opera and finally in London) was an anticlimax.

* * *

Klemperer's personality was always unstable, but the story of his American exile and eventual return to Europe is also one of triumph over impossible odds, with himself as his greatest enemy. In depressive phases, his music-making was often at its most inspired; when manic, he chased women, loitered in dives and brothels, squandered money, abused anyone who crossed him and composed prolifically. Managers, players, family and friends were all victims. Jobs disappeared; his wife and family were reduced to penury. A brain tumour was discovered and removed. There were heavy falls, broken bones, problems with his prostate and with cystitis. Yet in 1957, Legge could write that Klemperer's Beethoven concerts with the Philharmonia 'are going like wildfire. There has been nothing like this in London's musical life since Toscanini in the 1930s.'

If Klemperer was a catch for the Los Angeles Philharmonic Orchestra when he became principal conductor in 1933, he proved less than amenable to the New World context. An attempt by the orchestra manager's wife to crash the formality barrier swiftly came to grief. 'We'll have to call you "Klempie,"' she chirped. 'You may call,' came the reply, 'but I won't come.' José Rodriguez, a critic who became the conductor's friend, saw the situation exactly:

> In command of this rebellious and dispirited regiment is Otto Klemperer – a conductor of the highest achievements … a man who considers his function to be simply that of performing the finest music in the finest manner. And here is the rub, for in Southern California this is only half his job. His background has rendered him blind as a mole to the social aspects of his task.[5]

In effect, the Philharmonic was the private orchestra of a certain William Andrews Clark, who had aspirations as a conductor. In his dressing room after a Bach-Stravinsky-Beethoven concert, Klemperer was astonished to hear the 'Stars and Stripes' coming from the auditorium; it turned out that Clark had assumed the helm for an encore. Klemperer ordered his employer to drop the baton, an injunction that was needed again when, staying as a guest in Clark's house, he was propositioned by his entirely naked host.

There was also the inescapable annual chore of the Easter Sunrise Service at the Hollywood Bowl (and subsequently at the Forest Lawn Memorial Park, immortalized by Evelyn Waugh in *The Loved One*). The orchestra assembled in the dark, many wearing gloves against the pre-dawn cold; at Klemperer's command, their fingers had to produce the preludes to *Parsifal* and *Die Meistersinger*, after which, his religious sensibility deeply offended by the whole occasion, the maestro had to endure breakfast and Easter eggs with the management.

Klemperer regularly sought to escape the LA Phil, but he paid the price for his missionary zeal. In guest appearances with the New York Philharmonic in the autumn of 1935, he was plainly on trial as a possible successor to Toscanini. But he excelled only in those items by Mahler, Schoenberg and Berg from which the audience stayed away in droves. In the popular classics, he was considered too stolidly German, and he showed little concern for the tonal sheen that New York audiences regarded as the hallmark of fine playing. Heyworth describes his interpretations as having had 'an uncomfortable way of challenging accepted views of a piece of music in a city whose concert life had not been exposed to the purging fires of *die Neue Sachlichkeit*'. No voices called for his return, and, to Klemperer's chagrin, it was Barbirolli who eventually succeeded Toscanini in 1936.

In the same year, Klemperer returned to Europe to give the first Viennese performance of Berg's Violin Concerto, but later passed up the chance to give its first West Coast performance with Szigeti in 1945. (Not even Klemperer's advocacy could overcome the hostility to those modernist composers he still attempted to champion; as a result, his own interest in performing them slackened.) There were more concerts in Vienna and in Moscow with the 20-year-old Emil Gilels as soloist in Beethoven's Piano Concerto in C minor; and in Leningrad with Beethoven's *Eroica* and the Choral Symphony. He met Shostakovich and heard him play through his Fourth Symphony – Klemperer begged to be allowed to give its first performance outside the Soviet Union. Plans were

---

5. Heyworth, Klemperer 2, p. 73.

made, but Stalin's purges swiftly led to the withdrawal of all invitations to foreign conductors. Within two months, German troops had marched into Austria, and so, as Heyworth puts it, 'the spread of totalitarianism of the Left and Right finally brought to an end the chequered career Klemperer had been able to maintain in Europe since he left Germany five years earlier'.

For all his waywardness, Klemperer was still highly valued by the LA Phil, and in February 1938, the orchestra renewed his contract. Then disaster struck. Difficulty in maintaining his balance led to the diagnosis of a brain tumour. Its removal in September 1939 left him with partial paralysis of the right side of his face and body, and with his speech and hearing impaired. Worse still, his convalescence marked the onset of a particularly self-destructive manic phase. He began an affair with (Friedel) Maria Schacko, the 35-year-old wife of the conductor Maurice Abravanel. One night he brought Maria home, whereupon his wife, the long-suffering Johanna, walked out and threatened divorce. In a letter attempting to calm her down, Klemperer protested that he still loved her and – in a gambit worthy of Groucho Marx – added that he had not the slightest grounds for divorce.

The reckless behaviour continued in New York, where he had concerts to give. There, he attended early Mass, dashed off political tracts, went to Harlem, got beaten up and was put in a psychiatric clinic from which he quickly absconded. The police issued an eight-state alarm describing him as 'dangerous and insane'. Captured and thrown into gaol, he awaited rescue by his family. It was, as he remarked, just like Eisenstein in the last act of *Die Fledermaus*. To get his own way with a chamber orchestra of émigré Europeans – he demanded that they should stand up to play Bach – Klemperer produced what appeared to be a revolver, but turned out to be a water-pistol. The musicians, though understandably alarmed, were impressed by his conducting and stayed to perform. The first of the four concerts went well enough for *The New York Times* to praise, without irony, the 'wholesomeness and sanity' of the performances. Ernst Bloch remarked that 'Klemperer's musicality stood like a fortress in occupied territory, the sole part of his character to resist the devastating impact of his illness'. After making another scene at a rehearsal for a concert in January 1941, Klemperer walked out into a future in which he was unemployed and unemployable.

Back in Los Angeles, he became withdrawn, tight-fisted, cold and distant. Conductors like Bruno Walter and Georg Szell were in the ascendant, and despite the best efforts of Schoenberg and Stravinsky, there was no work for the maestro. Solace and intellectual sustenance were afforded by European exiles like Thomas and Heinrich Mann, Franz Werfel and Alma Mahler, Bertolt Brecht and Helene Weigel, Hanns Eisler and Lion Feuchtwanger, who 'had transformed what had been an intellectual desert into the temporary cultural capital of the German-speaking world'. But it was to be more than three years before sufficient stability returned for Klemperer, again with heroic support from wife and daughter, to resume his concert career.

On 24 June 1946, Klemperer became the first of the great émigré conductors to return to Germany. 'I have come to Baden to try to heal the wounds made by this terrible time', he told the orchestra. But his own wounds were far from healed, and his return to America was marked by a fresh upsurge in manic behaviour. Managers and performers were treated to the water-pistol and worse. He was robbed, beaten up and strapped to a bed in a sanatorium. No one could discover whether the mania was a physical result of the tumour operation or neurotic in origin – a conundrum that even Heyworth's research cannot explain.

Eventually it was Aladár Tóth, critic and then head of the Budapest Opera, who gave Klemperer his second chance. Hungary was still a relatively independent country when Klemperer arrived there in October 1947, following in the footsteps of Mahler and Nikisch as musical director of the Opera. It was the right job at the right time, bringing Klemperer back to opera and, above all, into a European milieu where his eccentricities strengthened rather than diminished his reputation. He composed furiously; some of his works with sung texts made no secret of his increasingly radical political views.

His compositions include songs, choral works (many testifying to his profoundly religious nature: he converted from Judaism to the Catholic faith in 1919), incidental music for *Faust* and the *Oresteia*, and at least three operas. Ferdinand Pfohl, reporting a recital in 1915 when a well-known singer was accompanied by Klemperer in a programme whose second half consisted of nine of his songs, complained that the composer-pianist:

> imposed his tyrannical will, indicating bar lines and entries by stamping his foot or an imperious nod of his head, relentlessly insisting on an idiosyncratic sense of rhythm without for a moment allowing the voice a right to its own development or self-enjoyment . ...[1]

But although Heyworth cites the divided reactions to performances of these works (usually under the composer himself), ranging from dismissal, through evasion, to acclaim, he is reticent about his own views.

Until the mid-1920s Klemperer generally followed Mahler's practice of retouching wherever the score failed to satisfy his own, composer's ear. In the late 1920s and 1930s he became much more *Werktreue*, while in his final period he again adopted a more empirical approach. Klemperer's attitudes to the score were constant only in the assumption that *he* knew what it was that the composer wanted to say – maybe not an uncommon attitude among conductors, but hard to account for in someone who strove so hard to be the music's servant rather than its master. Perhaps that is just the point, Klemperer regarding the composer, like the conductor, as an imperfect vessel through which the music had to pass.

* * *

As music director of the Budapest Opera it was perhaps understandable that Klemperer should identify with a regime that gave him the working conditions he needed, but as the Cold War intensified, this created problems when it came to travelling abroad. It did not go unnoticed that, while critical of Furtwängler's failure to dissociate himself from the Third Reich, Klemperer allowed himself to become an ornament of Hungary's developing totalitarian regime. For reasons that were, *au fond*, artistic, he had put himself on the wrong side of the political fence.

---

1. Heyworth, Klemperer 1, p. 103.

His performances continued to rub against romantic tradition, but now began to win praise for this very reason. 'If his *Eroica* was not "our" Beethoven,' wrote a Dutch critic of a 1947 concert with the Concertgebouw, 'in his choice of tempi and firmness of pulse, it was probably closer to "Beethoven's Beethoven".' The extravagant podium gestures of his earlier career relaxed into a less demonstrative semaphore. In Mozart's Prague Symphony in Berlin in 1948, it was noticed that his tempi were 'as fast as they always were ... but the relentlessness with which he formerly clung to dynamics and tempi is no longer so fierce and unyielding'.

Klemperer felt at home in East Berlin, where his friends Dessau, Bloch, Eisler and Brecht were now living, and he enjoyed working on *Carmen* at the Komische Oper with Walter Felsenstein (the first 'producer of genius' he had encountered since 1933). Mentally, however, Klemperer had already packed his bags, and when Felsenstein offered him the musical directorship of the Komische Oper, he declined. An escape route opened up in 1948 when he travelled to London for a concert of Bach, Stravinsky and Beethoven with the Philharmonia Orchestra, founded by Walter Legge as a pre-eminent recording ensemble for EMI. Further concerts in 1951 led to a recording contract with EMI, and Klemperer was finally appointed principal conductor for life of the Philharmonia in 1959 at the age of 74. His musicianship and wit endeared him to London musicians and if his view of Mozart was often too solid for Anglo-Saxon taste, as Heyworth claims, his performances of Bach, Beethoven, Brahms and Mahler with the Philharmonia had an irresistible *auctoritas*; he began to be spoken of as the leading Beethoven conductor of the day. As Desmond Shawe-Taylor well described it, Klemperer:

> does not linger and sentimentalize as Furtwängler did; nor does he, like Toscanini, subordinate everything to architecture and vital rhythm. His conception [of the *Missa Solemnis*] is noble, intensely musical, and satisfying.[2]

Klemperer's skies were never unclouded for long. In another manic phase, the septuagenarian's pursuit of a red-headed cellist looked all too like a rehearsal for the *Don Giovanni* he was to record in 1966. Complementary preparations included Italian lessons and a rereading of Kierkegaard's *Diary of the Seducer*. A bout of composition in 1962 produced an opera on *The Merry Wives of Windsor*, but composing was never his strong suit. Acknowledging receipt of a Symphony in Two Movements, Benjamin Britten saw no point in being tactful:

> I feel that your ideas are often very good. ... But, dear Doctor, I am not always so sure that the notes you have chosen are always the exactly right ones to express what is so clearly in your mind.[3]

Further punishments lay in wait, not least some terrible injuries from a fire caused by smoking his pipe in bed (the somnolent maestro had attempted to dowse his bedclothes with camphor spirit, which he had mistaken for water). The burns prevented him from

---

2. Heyworth, *Klemperer*, vol. 2, p. 260.
3. *Ibid*, p. 298.

conducting *Die Meistersinger* at Bayreuth – one of the greatest disappointments of his life – but he recovered well enough to conduct and produce *Fidelio* and *Lohengrin* at Covent Garden.

Although no longer performing much twentieth-century music, Klemperer took a lively interest in a number of younger composers and performers, Pierre Boulez, Daniel Barenboim and Jacqueline du Pré prominent among them. Visitors to his quarters in the Hyde Park Hotel were likely to be regaled with recordings of Tom Lehrer's 'Alma' and 'The Vatican Rag' with Klemperer joining in the refrain, 'Genuflect! Genuflect! Genuflect!'. At the same time he left the Catholic Church and returned to Judaism. His renewed spiritual strength yielded a series of remarkable concerts and recordings including Mahler's Seventh and Ninth Symphonies, *Das Lied von der Erde* (with Janet Baker and Richard Lewis) and Bach's B Minor Mass. But the indomitable energy was beginning to flag, and he retired in 1971. Tended by his daughter Lotte, Klemperer died on 6 July 1973, aged 88, and was buried in the Jewish cemetery in the hills high above Zürich.

Heyworth's superb documentation of Klemperer's long life reveals a complex, and often paradoxical, relationship between the conductor's personality, his achievements and the legend that has sprung from both. Some adjustment is now needed to Klemperer's reputation as a mighty musical intellect, as a magus with irrefutable insight into the works he played. In the German-speaking world, and even beyond it, his image is that of a torch-bearer of moral truth in and through music, a conductor with an 'uncanny ability to convey the idea as well as the sound'.

Yet one also recalls the wilfulness, even obstinacy that was so distinctive and so central a quality of his music-making. Those great performances were surely conjured not at all from the intellect but through Klemperer's indomitable will, a will usually locked in combat with the terrifying ups and downs – so well described by Heyworth – of his manic-depressive disposition. Pre-eminently, he was a man of instinct and feeling: an intellectual would have sought to explain and justify his diverse performing practice, his somewhat irrational preferences in the music of his own time. His was the supreme daemonic attainment of transmitting powerful feelings through music while having the audience believe that it was an irreproachably intellectual and moral experience that was on offer.

He could not have hoped for a more devoted and percipient chronicler than Peter Heyworth. Always alive to the broader political and cultural context, Heyworth's biography is a landmark contribution to the story of musical life in our century. It would be hard to imagine a fairer assessment of the conductor; here we have the triumphs and disasters, the idiosyncrasies and even some of the elusive greatness of Klemperer's conducting. But, in the end, posterity's only real access to his achievement is through his recordings. To these there could be no better guide than the 72 pages of Michael H. Gray's accompanying discography.

Illustration 1: Herbert von Karajan in reflective
mode: he believed that music was the better
part of the German soul.

Chapter Ten

Karajan: The Conductor as Supreme Being[1]

'One either makes music or politics,' Herbert von Karajan told his de-Nazification tribunal in Vienna in March 1946. They were his concluding words in an interrogation that had lasted two and a half hours. His chief examiner rounded off the proceedings by observing, 'I can't imagine today that even an artist can be completely unpolitical.' The verdict reflected that thought; Karajan could continue to perform as a conductor 'but not in a leading capacity'. If the tribunal of his fellow Austrians had hoped that this condition would chasten or restrain his Führer tendencies, they were mistaken.

In a way, the 'de-Nazification' of Karajan and other leading musicians was a fudge, reflecting the shared desire of the Allied Forces of Occupation and of the Austrians themselves that normal artistic service should be resumed as soon as possible. Music had kept everyone going through the war; its continuation offered therapy among the ruins, and for the vanquished and victors alike. In April 1945, days after the Soviet army took Vienna, the hastily appointed head of the Opera was commanded at gunpoint to

---

1. Source: 'The Conductor as Supreme Being', *Times Literary Supplement*, 20 November 1998, pp. 13-14.

give a May Day performance of *Le nozze di Figaro*. 'It is not possible', he stammered. 'Possible, is,' replied the Russian officer – and somehow or other a performance was scrambled together.

For the Americans, the truth about Karajan's involvement with the Nazis was assigned to the grey rather than black category, and so it has largely remained. The principal task that Richard Osborne has set himself, in his *Herbert von Karajan*,[2] is to ferret out the complex truth about a conductor whose work he has long revered. He acknowledges the help of Gisela Tamsen, a no less dedicated Karajanissary, who died in 1997, and to whose archive he has had exclusive access. Osborne himself first met Karajan in 1976, when commissioned to do an interview to help sell the maestro's latest set of the Beethoven symphonies. After a sticky start, the great man eased up and was sufficiently reassured to invite Osborne to a rehearsal in which the star turn was the 13-year-old Anne-Sophie Mutter in a Mozart violin concerto.

Osborne's aim is to illuminate, to understand, never rushing to judgement or approbation. His instinct is to treat 'Das Wunder Karajan' as a phenomenon, like that of Wagner, beyond all rational canons of censure – a cause for wonderment and despair that the timber of humanity, especially when touched by genius, should be so crooked. Not that this fair, if committedly partisan biographer (his book proves that such epithets are reconcilable), isn't able to raise an eyebrow from time to time. On 9 November 1938, the Kristallnacht, when, following the assassination in Paris of a German diplomat by a 17-year-old Polish Jew (the incident that inspired Tippett's *Child of Our Time*), Jewish shops were smashed and synagogues firebombed, Karajan had conducted *Tristan und Isolde*, for the second time in Berlin. The morning after, the streets littered with broken glass, smoke still billowing from a handful of half-gutted buildings, Karajan left for Aachen: 'The reviews of [this] second Berlin *Tristan* were calmer than the first batch,' Osborne notes, 'though no less adulatory. Did he pause to read the rest of the news that morning in Berlin?'

What Karajan might have done about it is another matter. The price for his meteoric career to date – in 1935, at the age of 27, he had been appointed Generalmusikdirektor at Aachen, the youngest opera-house director in Germany – had been membership of the Nazi Party and a degree of *Gleichschaltung*, though the de-Nazification tribunals were to acquit him of political collaboration with the Reich. This was a young man bent on carving a career and with precious little hope of doing so outside Germany. Like Furtwängler, Knappertsbusch, Jochum, Richard Strauss, Wilhelm Kempff and many others, he paid the price in the belief that music was the better part of the German soul, the one certain thing.

Walter Legge probably got it about right in remarking that 'Politics as such never interested Karajan – only musical politics of which he was … the supreme master'. Of course, the Nazis, caught up in their own appalling tangle of political barbarity and artistic aspiration, kept the conductors in their place, rather as electors and prince-archbishops had once done. Hitler was unimpressed by Karajan, finding his Wagner performances insufficiently 'German'. In 1942, Karajan was dismissed from his congenial

---

2. Richard Osborne, *Herbert von Karajan: A Life in Music* (London: Chatto and Windus, 1998).

post in Aachen. When he behaved less than obligingly after Heinz Tietjen, head of the Prussian theatres, had preferred Furtwängler rather than himself as conductor for a gala *Meistersinger*, his career was grounded. Tietjen's assistant, Prittwitz-Gaffron, explained to Richard Strauss – who cherished Karajan as an approved exponent of his own music – that he had been behaving like a 'screen goddess'. Osborne rightly discerns that a less forgivable sin was the true reason for Karajan's rustication, his marriage to the quarter-Jewish sewing-machine heiress Anita Gütermann.

This must count as one of the rare moments when something other than naked musical ambition was allowed to determine his behaviour. But where Karajan's first marriage to the operetta singer Elmy Holgerloef (1938) had foundered on the insatiable demands of his career, his second, to Anita, was to pay off in her help with his post-war progression. In due course there was to be a third wife, Eliette Mouret (a glamorous model), and children. But this did not dissolve a degree of ambivalence in his sexual preferences. As Osborne somewhat archly observes, 'many of his most intimate long-standing relationships were with men who matrimonially speaking were celibate'.

The trajectory of Karajan's career as a whole seems to epitomize the phenomenon of the twentieth-century conductor, his rise to unprecedented power and public acclaim, his complicity in the commercialization of musical culture. No other contestant was so perfectly equipped to fulfil the conductor's destiny in relation to Walter Benjamin's gloomy prognostications in his famous essay 'The Work of Art in the Age of Mechanical Reproduction'. For the 25-year-old Heribert Ritter von Karajan, as he was baptized, who had so idiomatically been billed as conducting the incidental music to Max Reinhardt's Salzburg production of Goethe's *Faust* in 1933, soon transmuted into the Herbert von K whose name was to be synonymous with the development of recording technology.

The Karajan whose brilliant precision was as well suited to the three-to-four-minute sides of 78s as Furtwängler's inspirational style was not, went on to master the LP, stereophony and quadrophony and to be there at the birth of digital and the compact disc. No aspect of the technological processes escaped him, and their possibilities influenced his music-making as much as its demands conjured new technical miracles. Nor would music's potential for film, television and video be lost on him. Here, too, he was the pioneer, obsessed, it often seemed, with immortalizing the art of musical performance.

Karajan's recreations off the podium were of a piece with his music-making – the exhilaration of the precise control exercised by the expert skier, the racing driver, the yachtsman and the pilot, in all of which he excelled. He was acutely conscious of his own physiology – his heartbeat, breathing, muscular activity – as touchstone for the rightness of music's tempo and rhythm. His ability to memorize scores and run them through to himself with split-second consistency seems to have been uncanny. Conveying this to an orchestra came as second nature. What was always more questionable was the infallibility of his bodily functions, his complicity in the myth of the conductor as Supreme Being.

Arriving late to conduct a live broadcast of *A Child of Our Time* in Turin in 1953, Karajan suddenly insisted, totally against the wishes of an aghast Tippett, on inserting an interval halfway through Part Two. Could an uncomfortable memory of the oratorio's origin in the horrors of Kristallnacht have caught him unawares? When Karajan performed Henze's *Sonata per archi* in 1959, the composer was left feeling mugged; it was as though his work had been 'assimilated into the work of the great Kapellmeister and his orchestra'. But then this was a man whom Osborne describes as only ever being impressed, and fleetingly at that, by two political teachers after 1945 – De Gaulle and Thatcher. One is scarcely surprised to learn that the only temporal authority for which Karajan entertained any real respect was the papacy. About musical rivals he was totally paranoid; nothing sprang him more swiftly from a sickbed than to learn that Barenboim or Mehta were ready to jump in. Near the end of his life, he warmed to Rattle and rang to discuss something at Salzburg, but when Sir Simon asked about period instruments, Karajan hung up on him.

What of the character and quality of the music-making? Osborne files assessments of every concert, opera performance and recording of any significance. The chronicle is as unsparing of the maestro's weaker efforts as it is eloquent in discerning praise of his finest. Wearisome, maybe, when encountered as critical staging posts embedded in the biographical narrative, but invaluable for later reference.

This life of Karajan is necessarily also that of the orchestras with which he worked, most particularly the Vienna Philharmonic and the Berlin Philharmonic, which, when occasion demanded, he did not hesitate to set against each other. (When the Berlin Phil gave him trouble at Salzburg, he punished them by flying in the Vienna band at his own expense.) The politicking that went into the management of these orchestras (and of the Vienna State Opera, of which Karajan was director from 1957 to 1964) is a story in itself, one that puts Britain's present agonies over the funding of opera, ballet and music in general into perspective. Is anything new? 'The situation in Vienna had become impossible,' writes Osborne of 1964: 'It was the politics of the madhouse, and the Opera itself was the principal victim.'

The one huge and shaming difference between then and now is that in Karajan's Berlin and Vienna the civic funding of the arts, the commitment to them as essential to the spiritual health and well-being of society, was seldom called into question. (*Der Spiegel* launched an assault on Karajan's eightieth-birthday festivities in 1988 by tactlessly asking its readers whether they weren't paying too much into the coffers of 'Der Finanz-Magier', the financial wizard.) The hassles then were Olympian squabbles not about money, but about which conductors and soloists were put before the public, which works were played, which operas performed.

There was also a darker side, but Osborne stops short of probing its murkier corners. This side is the extent to which our modern musical culture has been, and continues to be, manipulated for profit – always in the name of Art, it goes without saying. If Berlin and Vienna were generally happy to pour money into their musicians, this did not assuage the musicians' thirst for lucre, plainly reflected in their programming and the deals struck with recording companies. No surprise, when it was apparent to all that Karajan (never shy about money) was making a killing each time he lifted the baton and closed his eyes. Osborne is at his most readable when describing how Walter Legge secured Karajan for the Philharmonia and in the subsequent tussles between EMI and Deutsche Grammophon for his favours.

Karajan's involvement with the rise and rise of recording is expertly untangled by Osborne. If Karajan shaped the art of recording, it in turn shaped him – and the extent to which it influenced changes in his music-making has never been so keenly noticed and described. His initial goal was a set of recordings that the collector could play repeatedly, precisely because the frozen performance was free from 'interpretation'. That also meant free from individuality of reading – it was, inevitably, an aspiration towards classic, definitive performance – a claim that even Karajan came to renounce. But as recording techniques dramatically improved, concurrently with Karajan's own maturation as an artist, so did his approach. Where, in the early days, he had insisted on perfecting short takes, latterly he liked to record in long stretches – 20 minutes was not uncommon – happy to overlook the odd mistake against the greater gain of sustained tension and flow. Over the first two decades of the LP (roughly 1950-70) Karajan 'had swung 180 degrees from being fascinated by the possibilities of tape editing to seeing it as something to be avoided wherever possible'.

Ultimately, Karajan was ambivalent about recording, convinced that the chimera of perfection could only be caught on the wing in live performance. His old friend Raffaello de Banfield received an urgent summons (to Berlin in the 1970s) from Karajan to hear him conduct a performance of Stravinsky's *Symphony of Psalms*. It was a work Karajan had loved for 40 years, but only now felt he was on the brink of performing to his satisfaction. Banfield reluctantly cancelled his dinner engagement, the miraculous performance materialized – after which Karajan never conducted the work again.

Karajan's long career was indeed rich in paradox, contradiction, tergiversation and, above all, change and development in his approach to music. It is because Osborne never neglects to show Karajan's humanity and fallibility, his weaknesses alongside his strengths, that the book is important. Osborne's obvious admiration for his subject is everywhere evident. But he has no qualms about including opinions and assessments by those less impressed. It is not a book Karajan himself would have tolerated, though you sense that many of the close friends who have been among Osborne's sources will not be upset that he has tried to tell a rounded tale. Even his most fervent, faithful admirers and supporters seem to have recognized that there were never any simple truths about Karajan – the good and the bad were inextricably intertwined. For his second wife, Anita, he was self-centred, lonely, intolerant, incorruptible and at the same time a 'lovely man'. Menuhin offers one of the deepest insights in observing the increased depth of his music-making after his major back operation in 1975 (a stroke was to follow two years later): 'Music had been for him a means of advance; it was only later, when he began to suffer, that he underwent a sublime transfiguration.'

What Osborne gives us is essentially a chronicle-biography, rich in documentation, well organized, but never quite free from a lingering sense of gratitude for the privileged access he has enjoyed to the great man and his entourage. You have the feeling that he may have been caught up in writing a far longer book than he had originally intended. Having sprung the lid of Pandora's box, he is slightly disconcerted by the profusion of its contents, happy to arrange it all neatly into piles, deal expertly with the tractable bits, but finally hand the Karajan conundrum back to the reader.

Illustration 1: Conjuring orchestral fireworks: Sir Georg Solti.

Chapter Eleven

Solti: Still Climbing the Mountain[1]

Scarcely the most indecisive of men, Georg Solti was dithering about Lord Drogheda's offer of the musical directorship of Covent Garden and turned to Bruno Walter. 'You must accept,' Walter told him, 'we, the older generation of conductors, no longer conduct opera. You of the younger generation must carry on our tradition and pass it on to the next generation. You are the link.' Solti of course took the advice and, as he had promised at his first press conference, within a few years put Covent Garden in the first rank of international opera houses.

Something of the story of how this came about is to be found in an enjoyable memoir[2] – completed only hours before Solti's sudden death on 5 September 1997, just short of his eighty-fifth birthday. Far from being a valedictory autobiography, this is the book of a man still climbing the mountain, of a man believing he had advanced more during the last five or six years than in the previous 50, and with engagements through to the next century. Good health and the energy of talent and ambition kept him on track

1. Source: 'Making Music that Breathes', *Times Literary Supplement*, 2 January 1998, p. 18.
2. Georg Solti, *Solti on Solti: A Memoir* (London: Chatto and Windus, 1997).

through an immensely long career with few setbacks. Solti's break came in 1946 with his appointment as musical director of the Bavarian State Opera. Trained in Hungary as a pianist and conductor, his experience went no further than *répétiteur* work for Toscanini at Salzburg, and the conducting of a single *Figaro* in Budapest, plus a couple of *Werther*s in Geneva. Arriving in Munich by US Army jeep in the freezing cold, Solti was appalled by the devastated city. Germany being Germany, the opera had to go on. The Opera lay in ruins but a suitable house in the shape of the Prinzregententheater had somehow survived. Pending de-Nazification, not a single eminent native conductor was available, Furtwängler, Knappertsbusch, Clemens Krauss and Karajan all being banned from performing.

Into the breach, and not a little to his surprise, sprang Solti. Munich had at first declined his services, whereupon Stuttgart snapped him up for a *Fidelio* whose triumph (with the young Wolfgang Windgassen as Florestan) led to him being offered the musical directorship there. But when news of this *Fidelio* reached Munich, he was immediately invited back there to perform the same work with the Bavarian State Opera. This turned out to be his successful audition as musical director – a more important post than the one in Stuttgart would have been. The locals, anxious to reassert the supremacy of 'deutsch und echt', were pining for Knappertsbusch, but the 33-year-old Hungarian Jew won through. After a few years he was off to Frankfurt, where he could shape an ensemble to his own taste with none of the artistic interference and cultural politics to which he had been subject in Munich. He gives us tantalizing glimpses of meetings with Richard Strauss, Thomas Mann and Hermann Hesse, and of Theodor Adorno, who introduced him to the music of Bruckner and Mahler and persuaded him to tackle *Lulu* and *Moses und Aron*.

Solti's international career in opera concert and recording studio never looked back. He did indeed keep the music-making ideals of the early twentieth century thrillingly alive right through into the vicissitudes of the *fin-de-siècle* cultural market-place. He does not fail to credit his teachers Bartók and Kodály, Leó Weiner and Dohnányi, and charts his indebtedness to the great conductors from whom he learnt, including Toscanini, Walter, Klemperer, Busch and Kleiber. He always tried, he says, 'to combine strength with Furtwängler's freedom'. He has much to say about orchestras as ensembles of immensely gifted individuals, seeing his own 'specific talent' in being able to 'make any orchestra play to the limit of its capacity, but only if the players are willing to make an effort'. (He records the New York Philharmonic in 1957 as being unwilling, but that the magic mostly worked.)

It was the same with singers. He acknowledges his early work as a *répétitéur* as crucial. 'Working closely with singers, year after year, teaches you to make music in a way that breathes – to phrase properly, even in purely instrumental music.' For all his fame as a conjuror of orchestral fireworks and explosive *sforzandi* this was never at the expense of his singers, with whom he enjoyed a superlative rapport. I vividly recall attending rehearsals and performances of Mahler's Eighth Symphony during his 22-year love affair with the Chicago Symphony Orchestra. The eight solo singers had every reason to be terrified, but Solti ringed them round himself in a reassuring semicircle, cajoling Mahler's monster orchestra into a perfect balance with the soloists without any of them having to strain. 'Shut up! Shut up! *Piano*, please, *piano*! Listen to the singers. I will tell you when you can play *forte*!'

Not that Solti didn't have his sticky moments or vexatious half-hours. During King Marke's lament in Act Two of *Tristan* in Los Angeles, sung by a numbingly dull bass, a man in the audience cried out, 'That's enough!' This reduced both Solti and the orchestra to helpless mirth, for, as Solti admitted, the truth was out. Somehow, the act was brought to its conclusion. Not so during *Salome* in Paris, when Grace Bumbry left the stage before the Dance and never reappeared. Such was the audience's outrage that Solti nearly ended up with his own head on a platter.

At Covent Garden, he was indefatigably inquisitive, making direct demands not only on the musicians but also on everyone backstage. It was bitterly resented; he was called the 'Screaming Skull' and worse. But as he had learnt in Germany, it was the right way to energize morale and to secure fine performances. Gradually, people saw the point. At the end of the golden decade of his tenure, in 1971, the tribute he cherished most was that of the chief stage technician: 'You taught me how to make a theatre work properly – how to create a proper production. I hated you at first. I called you a Prussian Field Marshal, because you enforced discipline. But now I know what you were aiming at . …' Covent Garden's crisis of today [1998] is partly attributable to financial and political circumstances far distant from those in the 1960s, but it is unlikely to rectify itself until it can rediscover a music director to provide Solti-style leadership in every corner of the company. Even the most competent management will flounder without it.

Plainly this memoir is far from the whole Solti story. His wife, Valerie, coaxed it out of him with the threat that 'if you don't write a book, someone else will and you won't like it!'. Harvey Sachs is thanked for turning 'my Anglo-Magyar-Teutonic speech into understandable English' – but this has happily not muted the inimitable Solti voice, though how we miss his emphatic accent and gestures. When the full story comes to be told, it will have much to add, and a few errors to correct: the tenor Jess Thomas would not have been amused to find himself billed as 'Jeff'; Joseph II's remark about 'too many notes, dear Mozart' was reportedly made of *Die Entführung aus dem Serail*, not *Figaro*; Solti the Straussian would surely have known that *Elektra* was substantially complete before the composer acquired his Garmisch villa. Solti deserves a biographer as scrupulous and attentive to the political and cultural backdrop as Klemperer had in Peter Heyworth. For the moment, one can only be grateful that this very great conductor set down his own vivacious account of achievements that have immensely enriched the musical life of the twentieth century.

Part Four

Opera Backstage: The Dramaturg's Story

Illustration 1: Soprano Jill Gomez and the author, Covent Garden's first Dramaturg, photographed during an interval in a dress-rehearsal, 1990.

Chapter Twelve

Phantom at the Royal Opera[1]

As the Royal Opera House (ROH) staged its grand reopening in 1999, two of its former bosses filed conflicting accounts of its recent history.[2] Both John Tooley (1970-88) and Jeremy Isaacs (1988-97) describe the House's considerable achievements over the past half-century; and Isaacs' part in pushing through the magnificent rebuilding was heroic. What we still want to know is why things also went so cataclysmically wrong.

Isaacs had come to the job after six years as head of Channel 4 (he was, in fact, the founding chief executive), where, thanks to him, the performing arts had been given a good run – in one remarkable year the channel broadcast twelve operas. Sir Claus Moser, chairman of the ROH Board, had invited Isaacs onto it in 1985 and within three years he found himself general director. Tooley argues that the job

---

1. Source: 'How Long before Ofop Steps In?', *London Review of Books*, 16 March 2000, pp. 26-27.
2. John Tooley, *In House: Covent Garden, 50 Years of Opera and Ballet* (London: Faber, 1999), and Jeremy Isaacs, *Never Mind the Moon: My Time at the Royal Opera House* (London: Bantam, 1999).

needs theatrical experience, but Moser's Board took a different view, passing over the claims of music and theatre men like Humphrey Burton, John Drummond and Brian McMaster, and instead gambling that Isaacs would find a proper place for Covent Garden in a televisual age.

Isaacs knew that the House was adrift. He looked forward to bringing a sense of purpose and adventure to the programming, as I did when I agreed to join him in the new post of dramaturg. My own brief was to be 'involved in discussion of the planning and rationale of all … opera productions' and responsible for arranging lectures and other events. I had seen 'dramaturgy' at work in German theatres and knew something of what Edmund Tracey and Nicholas John had been doing at the English National Opera. No one did that kind of thing at Covent Garden, and the mail I received suggested that others, too, thought it was high time they started. Those in the House were less certain. An opera house is a trade- and craft-oriented place in which every seamstress and stagehand knows just how the show ought to go. Hiring an outsider to have a say in that was not altogether popular.

When Tooley stepped down in 1988 he'd been with the House since 1955, first as assistant to David Webster, the Liverpool department-store manager who'd built it up from its wartime use as a dance-hall, and then for eighteen years as general director. The high point of Webster's reign was the Georg Solti era (1961-71). Tooley presided over the rather lesser era of Colin Davis (1971-86). Things, indeed, began to fall apart when Davis' partnerships with Peter Hall and Götz Friedrich broke down. Tooley dutifully chronicles the years from 1947 to 1988, but only comes alive in his final 80 pages, with a disgruntled assessment of his successor. Isaacs for his part is critical, if not harshly so, of Tooley. He is, if anything, tougher on himself and disarmingly candid about some (but not all) of the things that went wrong. His tone is characteristically brisk and bullish, his account not short on pride that he achieved so much.

The one point on which Tooley and Isaacs are agreed is that the House has always been strapped for cash, and under Thatcher became impossible to manage sensibly. Public subsidy, as a proportion of income, was cut back from 56 per cent in 1980-81 to 37 per cent in 1991-92 – less than half what comparable Continental houses get. The House struggled to make up the shortfall with private sponsorship (up from 9 to 19 per cent over the same eleven years) and huge hikes at the box office (seat prices up by 126 per cent over the five seasons 1986-91, compared with a retail price index rise of 37 per cent).

The consequence of this was that wealthy donors had too much influence on policy, and that a great many people were priced out. The general impression – which did not wholly accord with the facts – was that the taxpayer was stumping up to subsidize the pleasures of the rich. (No one complained that the premium prices paid by the wealthy subsidized the cheaper seats.) Guardians of public money of every political colour from David Mellor and Gerald Kaufman (described by Isaacs as possessing 'toxic conceitedness') to Chris Smith were not amused.

How, people asked, was the 'income requirement' of the Arts Council's most voracious client arrived at? Were the singers' fees not excessive, did the stage crews not live the life of Riley? A succession of investigations by expensive consultants initially acquitted the House of poor housekeeping, though, as Isaacs' regime drew to its close, they did pick up on much that was wrong. In 1983, an investigation of both the Royal Shakespeare Company (RSC) and the ROH, commissioned by Thatcher from Clive Priestley, an adviser to the Cabinet Office, concluded that the House was efficiently run and should be more generously supported. A one-off increase in the grant followed, but Priestley's crucial recommendation, that the annual grant be pegged to inflation, was disregarded. Opera and ballet were luxuries that must be paid for by their audiences. Cash was now coming in from private and corporate sources, and seat prices went through the roof. For a short time, the books were balanced. But the upswing in self-generated income was taken by the government as reason to reduce public funding further. The recession of the late 1980s took its toll of the private sponsors. The House began to falter just as Isaacs' more adventurous repertory came on stream.

Tooley attributes the crisis to Isaacs' refusal to be deflected from his artistic goals. He himself had been careful not to programme anything that was likely to embarrass the House with the bank. But even so, during his last eight years in charge, it was in the black only twice, and that includes the year of the exceptional one-off rescue package secured by Priestley. Tooley had a fine record of play-safe productions, in which the world's best singers could appear without needing too much rehearsal. Ironically, it was thanks to Tooley's legacy (an artistic doldrums, according to his successor) that Isaacs could put on the modernist triumphs of Berio's *Un re in ascolto* and Birtwistle's *Gawain*. But there's no denying there were also some terrible Tooley-hatched turkeys: Andrei Serban's *Fidelio*, Bill Bryden's *Parsifal*, John Copley's *Norma*, the Lyubimov *Rheingold*. There were also bizarre mismatches between conductor, director and designer – something my own arrival was supposed to help correct.

Isaacs knew he had to do better, to restore a sense of excitement with more new productions, if possible commissioned from the new wave of British directors and designers who'd been ignored by the previous regime. It would be expensive, but he would somehow find the money. Tooley expresses surprise and dismay that Isaacs kept on so few of his own closest associates to help him achieve these aims – rash and ill-advised though they seemed. But this scarcely corresponds with the facts. So far as I'm aware, the only notable change was the replacement of Tooley's technical director with John Harrison, who was to work miracles with the moribund stage equipment and play a key role in devising the stage mechanics of the new theatre.

Isaacs did create one or two wholly new jobs, bringing in John Cox, for example, as director of productions. The hope was that a more carefully thought-out approach would result in a better alignment between the House's musical strengths and the theatrical side. There were, however, serious obstacles, one of which was Bernard Haitink, the music director recently appointed under Tooley. Haitink had come from Glyndebourne, where he had never had to conduct anything that taxed his limited understanding of opera as music theatre. He had apparently accepted the job at Covent Garden on the understanding that he would be able to conduct the *Ring*. No one was unduly concerned about the limited time he would be able to give to the House, or about the desirability of his being involved in the planning and production processes. He was a world-renowned orchestral conductor and that was enough. But of course it wasn't, and Tooley's appointment of Jeffrey Tate as principal conductor made little sense because his strengths and Haitink's were not complementary. Both were chasing the German repertory, leaving the Italian one to ad hoc guest conductors.

Lacking any distinctive theatrical taste of his own, Haitink became the victim of those who had to decide things for him. In Michael Waldman's unsparing television documentary *The House*, the hapless Haitink is seen to be flabbergasted as the head of the opera company, Nicholas Payne, tries to sell him the director Richard Jones' scheme for the *Ring*. In *Die Walküre*, Fricka would arrive not in a chariot drawn by rams – as specified by the composer – but in a collapsible car. 'What can I say?' Haitink sighs, and the show goes ahead. What he made of the obscenely gross, nude Rhinedaughters or bag-lady Norns is not hard to guess. Before that, in his first *Ring*, he had endured Yuri Lyubimov's crass *Rheingold* (Lyubimov had been Haitink's own choice) and, when that was wisely aborted by Isaacs, the claustrophobic vision, inspired by the Washington subway, of Götz Friedrich's second-hand *Ring*, which was hastily pulled in to fill the gap.

Haitink also had to keep his head well down through Bill Bryden's 1988 *Parsifal* (another own goal: he'd imagined that the director of *The Mysteries* would be just the man for Wagner's sacred festival drama). He turned down the idea of a collaboration with Elijah Moshinsky (one of the few people with whom he might have struck up an understanding partnership) on the grounds that Moshinsky's positioning of the chorus in *Lohengrin* had not made the most of their volume.

Had Haitink been working at the Met these problems wouldn't have arisen – there, Isaacs observes, all that is usually demanded of the *mise-en-scène* is that it be 'lavish'. Isaacs, quite rightly, had other ambitions: but they were never going to fit in with Haitink. Another serious problem was that Haitink showed little interest in the day-to-day affairs of the House, nor did he take the lead in artistic policy and planning. Nominally, he was music director (and would be until 2002), which ought to have meant that he was boss in his own theatre, as Solti had so notably been. But he wasn't, and although the orchestra loved him, his effect on morale in general was not good. Nor, when the crisis deepened, was he there to talk to the world and win sympathy for the House.

All of this meant that it was necessary to have an administrative head of the company who was also, in effect, its artistic head. Isaacs' plan had been to bring one in from outside, which would have involved 'dropping' Paul Findlay, who after years of helping to make things work for Tooley, was at last in the driving seat as director of opera. When Isaacs mentioned his plan to Tooley over breakfast at the Savoy, a snag emerged. Aware that Haitink had decided that the experienced Findlay was someone he could rely on, Tooley told Isaacs: 'Keep Findlay and you have Haitink, or you lose both. That you cannot afford.' It was advice Isaacs had to swallow.

My own job as dramaturg and John Cox's as production director were, I suspect, intended at least in part to curb Findlay's excesses and help sift his good ideas (of which there was never any shortage) from the bad. Isaacs set up an artistic planning group, chaired by himself with Haitink, Findlay, the casting director Peter Katona, Cox and me as members. When we met we reviewed the future schedule and discussed ideas for new productions. Haitink was seldom present, nor was anyone else from the music staff. On the rare and refreshing occasions when Jeffrey Tate was there, lots of ideas were aired. But the group was treated as advisory, few decisions were taken and nothing was minuted. When his proposals were contested, as they often were, Findlay insisted that he discuss the matter privately with Isaacs later, and Isaacs acquiesced. When Cox or I had doubts about Findlay's schemes, we were overruled.

After the first three instalments of the Friedrich *Ring*, it was agreed at the usual post-production meeting that we should draft some notes on the production to be sent to Friedrich. The draft was sent to Haitink for his comments. 'I feel I must warn you', he replied, 'that should this list of alterations actually be mailed to him, the opera house can surely … accept the fact that Götz will not return to Covent Garden. In any event, I do not wish to be associated with such a letter.' So it wasn't sent and more's the pity, not least because I knew Götz well enough to be sure he'd have been glad to have our comments and to take them seriously.

I tremble to recall the *Fidelio* of 1990, in which the director, Adolf Dresen, could not be dissuaded from rewriting the German dialogue in a fatuous attempt to give it 'relevance'. He got his come-uppance at a rehearsal from the conductor, Christoph von Dohnányi. Dresen was spending so long making a hash of the chorus blocking that Dohnányi took control of the stage as well as the pit, leaving Dresen to prowl around at the back of the stalls. Why Findlay wanted to revive this *Fidelio* is incomprehensible, as is the fact that essential changes to the production were forbidden in the interest of remaining faithful to Dresen's wretched concept of the opera, even though Dresen himself did not return for the revival.

In the end, Isaacs disposed of Findlay and brought in Nicholas Payne from Opera North, as he had always wanted to, but by then it was too late. By laying off staff (myself included), constricting the repertory and slashing budgets, the House was pulled back from a deficit approaching £4 million; but irreversible damage had been done in those first four years of Isaacs' regime. Much on the stage was still of high quality, yet it was quite evident that too little had been done to forestall trouble. It wouldn't be right to attribute the House's entire financial plight to artistic recklessness but that did play some part. On the other hand, Isaacs isn't wrong to insist that the bold programming, with its balance between crowd-pleasers and rarities, kept the box office buoyant when the high prices might have sunk it.

Through all this, Isaacs was pushing ahead with the immensely troublesome development plans, which involved temporarily closing the opera house and devolving the second ballet company to Birmingham. Again, I think this was right. What is hard to understand is why he made life so difficult by taking a confrontational stance with the media and with the politically sensitive – and doubtless exasperating – keepers of the public purse. It was one thing to slash the freebies to the great and the good, quite another to rob critics of their second ticket, deny them open questions at a crucial press conference, fire Ewen Balfour, his popular and respected head of PR, appoint a new PR chief in the shape of the phone-slinging Keith Cooper and allow unconditional access to the cameras that put the House on television in January 1996.

Maybe it is some consolation to Isaacs that when Lord Chadlington, the head of Shandwick, one of the most successful PR firms of modern times, assumed the board chairmanship in 1996, he, too, cocked up in this direction. It may be that there is something about running an opera house that goes to the head of almost everyone who comes in from outside and thinks they can do it – and in that sense Tooley's insistence on theatre experience as a requisite in an opera-house boss makes sense. With hindsight nothing in the adversarial Thatcherite climate was more important than getting public perceptions right. The House took far too long to learn that you put the artists in the shop window and keep everyone else out of sight.

Isaacs would perhaps have done better if he had taken the full measure of the resistance to a Royal Opera House that swallowed a lion's share of the arts budget but seemed to be so prodigal in its management and so exclusive in its clientele. He did fight hard to win recognition for the House's thriving programme of children's education, but the press never really wanted to know, and the Arts Council crassly continued – as it would continue to do – to bang on about finding new audiences and increasing 'access'. Isaacs did make efforts to give the House the accessibility that can only come from exposure on television – in 1991-92 3.3 million viewers tuned in to five productions. But it was not enough, and his inability to crack the in-house union problems – essential if the cost of televising shows was not to be prohibitive – did not help.

I often wonder whether it wouldn't have been better to have had a major clear-out at the end of the Tooley regime, thus enabling the fresh start that only the catastrophe of closure later made inevitable. The trouble was that Isaacs simply didn't know enough about running an opera house to have the confidence to hard-prune the theatre as he found it. Both he and Tooley give accounts of the chaos that descended after Isaacs' early departure (supposedly to give his short-lived successor Genista McIntosh a free hand). In all this one error of judgement was followed by another. But it has to be said that Isaacs and his board were not totally to blame: the finger also points at the Arts Council and the government.

Isaacs had reason enough to be exasperated with the Arts Council. It can't have been easy trying to negotiate with George Christie, chair of the Council's music panel, from whose Glyndebourne the House had filched not only Haitink but, more painfully, the fund-raiser Alex Alexander. Whether he would have got more cash had he been quietly persistent rather than confrontational is an open question. Maybe if he'd been even tougher, if he'd cancelled performances and offered his resignation unless he was given adequate core funding (a strategy successfully deployed by the RSC at the Barbican some years before) he'd have won through, or at least gone down in glory. Had the Council in turn had any understanding of what Isaacs might be able to do for the House, and supported him, it could have been a different story. But the Council had become the timid agent of the government's policy for Heritage and was no longer championing its clients' needs against Whitehall's parsimonious philistinism.

That the House has survived its troubles is due not to a visionary public arts policy but to Lottery largesse and munificent donors like Lord Sainsbury and Vivien Duffield, whose patience and enthusiasm stayed the course. What happens now [2000] is anyone's guess. It has taken an American chief executive, Michael Kaiser, to restore a semblance of order. He has the advantages of experience – having rescued three American ballet companies from the brink of extinction – of being a foreigner (that always helps in opera) and of coming totally fresh to the House. But there still isn't any palpable sense of artistic purpose. We must hope that Antonio Pappano will be a hands-on music director and that Elaine Padmore, the director of opera, will devise an exciting repertory: she has esoteric tastes (a very good sign) and is certainly not in opera for its glamour.

What kind of House it will be is critically dependent on what its paymasters want of it. In populist Britain, public subsidy carries populist imperatives. Access and availability can be assisted, but never satisfied, by television and big-screen relays: it is seats in the theatre that people are after and there are only 2,200 of those. Finding new audiences and making more seats available at lower prices will only exacerbate the frustration. And those lower prices mean more subsidy, not less. Moreover, it seems that there may be times when as few as 20 per cent of the seats will be available for public booking, the rest being reserved for the 19,000-strong 'Friends' (subscription £55) and the wealthy patrons. What kind of House those patrons want – and will have to be given – is anyone's guess, but it is more likely to be *Carmen*, *La bohème* and *Swan Lake* than *Gawain*, the cancelled *Le Grand Macabre* or new choreography by William Forsythe or Twyla Tharp.

Fresh from New York, where the arts are funded predominantly by 'philanthropists', Michael Kaiser knows all about this – though I don't doubt the altruism and adventurous taste of some benefactors. Without an adequate level of public funding the House will slip slowly but surely towards privatization. (The 'Royal' connection is a nonsense, useful only as a draw at fundraising galas.) It will be leased to entrepreneurs – just as used to happen before the birth of the Arts Council. Cameron Mackintosh and Raymond Gubbay are waiting in the wings, but Victor and Lilian Hochhauser have beaten them to it. In July and August this year they will be presenting the Royal Ballet's summer season and the Kirov Opera at Covent Garden. How long before the announcement of a government regulator? 'Ofop' sounds about right.

Illustration 1: Kenneth Woollam in the title role of Rienzi in ENO's 1983 production by Nicholas Hytner. The representation of Rome by models distanced the 'historical' context, while the portrayal of Rienzi as a modern dictator suggested the actualité of Wagner's third opera. This *Rienzi* was one of several mini-budget semi-staged productions of rarely performed works which showed ENO at its adventurous best.

Chapter Thirteen

Blood on the Carpet[1]

English National Opera in retrospect

London's English National Opera (ENO) has been in existence in one guise or another for nearly 130 years. Its story, by and large, is that of operatic life in England since the Victorian era. Jeremy Sams, witty translator for today's ENO, once said that opera appealed to the British precisely because it was foreign and sexy. Don't spoil the musical magic and the frocks by compelling us to pay attention to the words: let's just join Dr Johnson and revel in the 'exotic and irrational entertainment'. But that has never been the way with ENO. From Emma Cons and Lilian Baylis' idealistic dream in the 1890s of providing 'opera for everybody', down to the business-model ENO of today, the idea has always been that opera is living drama, intensified by music, and that unless you get the words you're not getting it at all. This, as Susie Gilbert explains in

---

1. Source: 'Blood on the Carpet', *Times Literary Supplement*, 1 January 2010, pp. 3-4.

her impressive chronicle, was important to the indomitable founding ladies.[2] Cons and her niece Baylis were missionaries, with equal commitments to art, religion and social reform. They believed that the diversions of the wealthy should be stripped of their foreign mystique and opened up to all as recreation that would get people to examine and improve their lives. 'Wholesome amusement', wrote a campaigning journalist in 1861, would lift costermongers out of 'the moral mire'.

For the first 60 years of ENO's life, Shakespeare, dance and lectures were equal partners with opera. The much-loved Old Vic theatre, just south of Waterloo and close to the tenements of Victorian London's workers, became the company's first home. Finance came from public appeals and from the private purse of Cons, until her death in 1912, and thereafter from Baylis. Wages and backstage conditions were abysmal, ticket prices kept as low as could be. The quality of performance was doubtless variable. Baylis asked little more of performers than that they stand and deliver. When the first combined Shakespeare/opera season was run in 1914-15, it was the greater popularity of *Carmen*, *Lohengrin* and *Don Giovanni* that paid for the plays. After the war there was a fresh momentum, with the Old Vic putting on all 36 of Shakespeare's First Folio plays between 1920 and 1923. Baylis strengthened her hand by bringing in the conductor Lawrance Collingwood and the Cambridge professor E.J. Dent to advise on opera repertory, and the baritone Clive Carey to enliven stage presentation. The derelict Sadler's Wells theatre in Finsbury, north of the Thames, was refurbished to become the home of the operatic part of the Baylis enterprise.

Through the 1920s the 'poorer classes' were gradually supplanted, so that in 1932 the *Radio Times* could report a knowledgeable audience of teachers, students and enthusiasts, 'scores under their arms, waving their coffee cups and arguing about the performance'. The Vic-Wells' great reformer of the 1930s, Tyrone Guthrie, kicked against Baylis' faith in art as social engineering, insisting that theatrical professionalism was what counted. He disliked the still-prevalent Victorian notion of the proscenium stage as framing an illusory other world. Following William Poel's anti-Irving initiative of the 1890s, he returned to the naked *actualité* of the Elizabethan stage while at the same time opening up a new world with his modern-dress *Hamlet* of 1937. Unable to go so far with opera, which he never saw as part of the 'native cultural tradition', he believed that the answer was always to direct it as living drama, just like a play, and not to allow it to become a concert in costume. Dent's mission was the opening up of German, Italian, French and Russian opera by performing it in translations that he himself supplied. Guthrie's suggestion that Rudolf Bing might run the Wells was swiftly scotched on the urging of Dent, who, for all his Continental leanings, had a deplorable anti-Semitic streak and was seriously worried by the prospect of German Jews taking over opera in Britain.

Baylis' original aims seem to have come closest to fulfilment during the Second World War, after her death in 1937. There were no performances at Sadler's Wells after September 1940, but public subsidy was granted for the first time in 1941. Guthrie managed to get no fewer than five Vic-Wells opera and ballet companies out on tour, typically with a tiny cast and 'orchestra' of five, visiting small mill towns in Lancashire

    2. Susie Gilbert, *Opera for Everybody: The Story of English National Opera* (London: Faber, 2009).

and Yorkshire. Well-attended children's matinees were given in Wigan, but hardly anyone turned up for *The Barber of Seville* in the Black Country's Dudley because, says Gilbert, 'they were saving up for the Christmas pantomime'.

The story of how Sadler's Wells separated itself from the Old Vic and thrived at Rosebery Avenue after the war under the inspirational direction of, first, Norman Tucker and then Stephen Arlen is well, if perhaps too cursorily, told. Gilbert is always aware of the wider context in which the growth of opera and ballet at Sadler's Wells and Covent Garden was dependent on burgeoning public subsidy. Inevitably, demand kept well ahead of the available funding, Norman Tucker making sure that Sadler's Wells stayed in the red in order to suck as much as possible from the Treasury (where he had once worked). The Arts Council, created by John Maynard Keynes in 1945, was supposed to bring a degree of discipline to state patronage and to some extent it succeeded in this aim. The tentative claims of the 'native cultural tradition' had received an enormous boost with the arrival of Benjamin Britten's *Peter Grimes* at Sadler's Wells in June 1945. On this foundation, the 1950s and 1960s were to become glory days for Sadler's Wells. Tucker pressed on with opera as 'radical theatre' by bringing in Michel Saint-Denis, George Devine and Glen Byam Shaw from the Old Vic. *Katya Kabanova* with Amy Shuard, introduced to the company and conducted by Charles Mackerras in 1951, was a revelation to most critics (though not to the unimpressed Ernest Newman), but sold few seats. Tucker nevertheless persisted with Janáček, over time winning the public round so that the introduction of his operas became one of the company's most impressive achievements.

I had my own first experience of live opera in 1959 when I bicycled the twelve miles from Rugby to see the Wells on tour at the Coventry Hippodrome. I still vividly recall the thrill of the violin figurations in the overture to *Tannhäuser* heard from a seat very near the front, and then Ronald Dowd in the title role in Anthony Besch's traditional pictorial staging – quaintly described by Gilbert as 'tactful'. The conductor was Colin Davis, whom I was lucky enough to meet afterwards in the theatre bar. He said he was meant to be rehearsing *Oedipus Rex* during the mornings but had unfortunately forgotten his score. So the next day I biked over again, taking my own score for him to borrow and catching Rossini's *Cinderella* in the evening. Davis was touched and grateful, posting it back to me some days later with a nice note. With hindsight I can't believe that the company wouldn't have themselves conjured up a score, but the ruffled pages of my copy suggested that it may well have served its turn for him on the podium. So Sadler's Wells became for me and thousands of others a gateway into opera, at affordable prices whether on tour or back in Rosebery Avenue. Michel Saint-Denis' stunning production of *Oedipus Rex* opened the following year.

Such repertory did not always go down well outside London. A Brigadier Hargreaves complained, 'Why do we have to fill up the touring rep with things like *Odious Rex* and the *Mackerras Case*?' I myself returned again and again for fine performances of the classic repertory and to be stretched by less familiar fare: *Mahagonny, Attila, The Makropulos Case, From the House of the Dead* and exciting works given by the New Opera Company, among them Henze's *Boulevard Solitude*, Szymanowski's *King Roger* and Shostakovich's *The Nose*. This education culminated in Reginald Goodall's *Mastersingers* in 1968, which I must have seen three or four times. It was a watershed in the fortunes of the Wells (1,499 seats), precipitating its move to the very much larger

Coliseum (2,354 seats), where Wagner and the grander works of Verdi were going to sound so much better. Inevitably, this brought to a head the long-standing tension between the Wells and Covent Garden, the latter falling under threat because of the proximity of the two theatres.

Susie Gilbert unravels the tortuous story of how that tension was managed, and of the political pressures to rehouse the company in a purpose-built theatre far away on the South Bank. While the company remained at Sadler's Wells it was relatively easy for people to accept it as the London equivalent of Paris' Opéra-Comique and Berlin's Komische Oper, giving medium-scale works in the vernacular with British and Commonwealth singers, while Covent Garden did the grand stuff in its original language with international casts. The move to the Coliseum compelled both companies to re-evaluate themselves, though the greater burden fell on English National Opera (as the company became in 1974). Its singers had to learn to make themselves heard in the largest theatre in the West End, and there was a loss of intimacy for the medium-sized repertory. ENO's strategy under, first, Stephen Arlen (until 1972), then Lord Harewood (until 1985) and thereafter Peter Jonas (until 1993), was to play to its strength of presenting opera as theatre in the vernacular, winning laughter in comedies and visceral shocks in the more violent works. In this there was an embodied censure of the Covent Garden audience's taste for sumptuous, undemanding entertainment. ENO's provocative stagings were an implicit condemnation of the operatic taste of the wealthy in much the same way as the severely abstract Bolshevik stagings of 1917-23 had been of the imperialist aesthetic of Tsarist Russia.

Harewood wanted operas to be 'made real in terms of contemporary anxieties, taboos and shibboleths'. So in came German directors Joachim Herz and Harry Kupfer from the Komische Oper, and British and American directors such as David Pountney and David Alden, excited as they were by what they'd seen on the Continent. This heralded an overdue awakening of British opera-goers to the radical reappraisal of performance that had been going on abroad since Meyerhold in Russia (from 1909), Toscanini at La Scala (from 1923) and Klemperer at the Berlin Kroll (1927-31). Things took off with the arrival in early 1979 of Mark Elder as music director and in 1980 of Pountney, whose seventeen productions were to include iconoclastic versions of *Rusalka*, *Orpheus in the Underworld* (designed by Gerald Scarfe, who put Margaret Thatcher on stage as 'Public Opinion'), *Carmen* (set in a breaker's yard), *Hansel and Gretel*, *The Queen of Spades* and *Lady Macbeth of Mtsensk*. It was farewell, meanwhile, to the old-style naturalism of ENO stalwarts John Copley and Colin Graham. Elder raised the lacklustre standard of the orchestra by replacing many of its players. He and Pountney campaigned against opera as 'a Fortnum and Mason window', insisting it should have a 'healthy vulgarity and terrifically wide range of appeal'. The bracing interrogation of the Pountney and Alden productions (by no means always as popular as they hoped) was balanced with gentler but no less potent transformations from Jonathan Miller (a Mafioso *Rigoletto*, 1982, and a Savoy Hotel romp of a *Mikado*, 1986) and Nicholas Hytner (*Xerxes*, 1985, and *The Magic Flute*, 1988) which have had a long life.

Gilbert reveals that Pountney's confrontations with the 'audience's susceptibilities' were not always to the liking of his generally supportive boss, Lord Harewood, concerned as he had to be about the mounting cost of the revolutionary programming. Sharing his concerns was the Arts Council, now under Thatcher's axe man, William Rees-Mogg, which raised a very old and silly spectre of ENO and The Royal Opera sharing a single theatre. (This was the critical moment when the Arts Council swung from being the defender of the publicly funded theatres to taking on the role of stern policeman.) Peter Jonas, taking over from Harewood in 1985, was more in tune with the goals of what became known as the 'Powerhouse' artistic directorate at ENO. At this time of great financial pressure, Jonas had the courage to deride Fortnum and Mason productions such as *Comte Ory* and *The Pearl Fishers*, which had somehow crept into his nest and were enjoying full houses. Tarred with the same brush was *The Magic Flute*, which, Hytner said, 'delighted audiences, but backstage this was a badge of shame'. In *Power House* (1992), the retrospective book celebrating their adventures, Jonas, Pountney and Elder wrote of having happily driven the Mercedes:

> on the wrong side of the road, put a few dents in the body work and filled the boot with muddy Wellington boots (not to mention suitcases, trilbies, wonky bedsteads, dark glasses and other gnomic properties).[3]

A heavy price was paid for the Powerhouse revolution. By 1993, when Dennis Marks took over from Jonas, and Sian Edwards became music director, there was a huge financial deficit. However nominally appealing the idea of a 'people's opera house' may have been to Tony Blair's first culture secretary, Chris Smith, the government couldn't bear the cost of funding it. Smith revived the notion that Covent Garden should become a 'hosting house' for performances by the opera and ballet companies of both The Royal Opera and ENO as 'equal partners'. Was he surprised when Richard Eyre's subsequent report, which he had commissioned, forthrightly rejected any such drastic reduction of ballet and opera provision in the capital? There was yet more government pressure to curb ENO's activities and move it to a smaller theatre away from the West End. Marks fought as well as he could, but retired from the field in September 1997. Next into battle arrived the well-armed Nicholas Payne and the conductor Paul Daniel, who rallied the audience against the threat of possible closure with post-performance speeches from the stage. Winning a reprieve, Daniel proved a strong music director, though Payne's own quietly sage taste in adventurous theatre (bringing in David McVicar for *Alcina* and *The Rape of Lucretia*) deserted him when he hired the Spanish director Calixto Bieito for despoliations of *Don Giovanni* and *A Masked Ball*. It must have been hard for Payne to accept that the big successes on his watch were revivals from previous eras – Hytner's *Xerxes* and *Magic Flute*, and Miller's *Mikado* and *Rigoletto*.

The deep trouble was that Payne, who had been forging ahead with the restoration of the theatre, didn't get on with the investment banker Martin Smith, who had been chairman since 2001. To wide dismay, Payne was ousted by Smith in the summer of 2002. As Gilbert observes, this marked a sea change in the direction of the company when it passed from artistically knowledgeable bosses to managerial accountants. There followed a period of serious demoralization and compulsory job losses, to which the

---

3. Nicholas John (ed.), *Power House: The English National Opera Experience* (London: Lime Tree, 1992), p. 16.

chorus responded by staging a protest outside the office of Gerry Robinson, now the Arts Council's chairman. They sang the 'Chorus of the Hebrew Slaves' from *Nabucco* and 'Defend Our Homes and Children' from *Khovanshchina*. Robinson described it as 'the most beautiful protest' he had ever heard. Smith eventually replaced Payne in 2003 with Sean Doran, who had directed festivals (Belfast and Perth) but had no experience of running an opera company. It was on his watch that the newly established Lottery Fund came to the rescue, enabling the Coliseum to reopen in February 2004 at a cost of £41 million, of which £23 million came from the Lottery and £18 million from private donations. Doran's tenure, however, was far from happy. His departure in 2005 proved no less controversial than his arrival had been when, without advertising the posts, the board replaced him with the twosome of Loretta Tomasi, former finance director, as chief executive, and John Berry, formerly in charge of planning, as artistic director. Thereafter, and with Edward Gardner as music director from 2007, things appear to have steadily improved. Against all odds, both Covent Garden and ENO managed to rebuild their beautiful theatres to near universal acclaim, however much blood may have been spilt on their backstage carpets.

Gilbert has a distinguished track record as an archival researcher (working on her former husband's biography of Winston Churchill) and her long book is meticulously documented. She has read every minute of every management meeting and questioned many living actors in the drama, though by no means all she should have. She gives a fair picture of ENO's development and the problems that have bedevilled it, much of it difficult to unscramble. The downside, unfortunately, is that the 700 pages are not an easy read. Too many of them are written in the language of a judicious civil servant, concerned lest any crucial fact be left out, although, as it happens, many facts are omitted: the list of first performances is skeletal, lacking the names of conductors, directors, designers and singers, the latter all too seldom given their due. A chronology would have been helpful. The reportage of board meetings and political and financial negotiations hangs heavily on the narrative. It is always hard to re-create theatrical performance on the page, and Gilbert does her best by quoting from press reports as she inevitably must, even honouring 'The Critics' with an appendix of their own. But few of the performances that I can personally recollect across the past half-century spring to life. Gilbert must surely herself be a fan of ENO and have seen many of their productions. It is a shame that she couldn't have given us some idea what she thought of them.

Illustration 1: Michael Tippett, photo montage by J. S. Lewinski, June 1977.

Chapter Fourteen

Michael Tippett on Opera[1]

A Conversation with the Composer

Sir Michael Tippett's fourth opera *The Ice Break* had its first performance on 7 July 1977, at the Royal Opera House, Covent Garden, conducted by its dedicatee, Sir Colin Davis. In a conversation with the author at the composer's home in Wiltshire, the 72-year-old Tippett reflected on a lifetime's preoccupation with music and drama.

As a student at the Royal College of Music in the early 1920s, Michael Tippett soon became involved as a *répétiteur* in ambitious undertakings in the college's tiny Parry Opera Theatre. The works in which he took part included *Pélleas et Mélisande*, Charpentier's *Louise*, the first performance of Vaughan Williams' *Hugh the Drover,* and *Parsifal* with the still young Adrian Boult ('we just performed the whole damn thing in two nights'). Tippett queued for five hours to hear the veteran Nellie Melba in *La bohème* – and some years later appeared for the fun of it on the Covent Garden stage

---

1. Source: 'The Composer as Librettist: a Conversation between Sir Michael Tippett and Patrick Carnegy', Times Literary Supplement , 8 July 1977, pp. 834-35.

as an extra in *Die Meistersinger von Nürnberg* during the General Strike because, so he says, the guardsmen were not allowed to: 'I just walked on and lifted my hat, or cap or whatever it was, at the right moment.'

Tippett was drawn as strongly to the theatre of words as to opera – and remained so. He was as struck by the political theatre of Ernst Toller as he was by Ibsen and the expressionist plays of Strindberg, and he was at the first performances of Shaw's *Back to Methuselah* – a bizarre echo from which appears in *The Ice Break*. His own first ventures as a theatre composer were an adaptation in 1927-28 of eighteenth-century ballad-opera *The Village Opera* ('a self-given lesson in some of the problems') and a second ballad-opera, *Robin Hood* (1934) with texts adapted by 'David Michael Penniless' (pseudonym for David Ayerst, Michael Tippett and Ruth Pennyman) written for the Ironstone miners of Cleveland in Yorkshire.

These were followed by two children's operas, *Robert of Sicily* (1938) and *Seven at One Stroke* (1939), both with texts by Christopher Fry, who had been English master at the prep school where Tippett had taught French for a while. Both of these pieces came out of working with children's choirs of the Royal Arsenal Co-operative Society: 'We had about fifty children in each choir so that it was possible to produce fifty children against one trumpet.' The musical basis was again folksong material, but although Tippett said that these works are 'too naive to be looked at now', he was no less firm that 'Fry knew what he was up to'.

Tippett's first major dramatic project emerged not as an opera but as the oratorio *A Child of Our Time* (1939-41). This work was written in response to the pogrom that had followed the shooting in Paris of a German diplomat by a young Polish Jew whose mother had been persecuted by the Nazis, and it was here that he first crystallized a music of passionate humanitarianism. He had approached T.S. Eliot, whom he knew and who exercised a formative influence on his thought, about a text for the oratorio, but on the poet's advice eventually decided to write his own words. This he continued to do, for reasons that will emerge, with the four operas that followed: *The Midsummer Marriage* (1946-52); *King Priam* (1958-61); *The Knot Garden* (1966-70); and *The Ice Break* (1973-76). One more opera was to follow, *New Year*, also to words of his own. This was premiered at the Houston Grand Opera in 1989 and first given in the UK by Glyndebourne Festival Opera in 1990.

* * *

Patrick CARNEGY (PC): How did *A Child of Our Time* begin?

Michael TIPPETT (MT): It was going to be an opera originally, and not on that subject at all. I was thinking of doing an opera on the Easter Rebellion and I studied a vast amount of Irish history, which I knew inside out. The Easter notion and other things are still there in the *Child*. But I then realized it wasn't going to come out in that way, so that I shifted sharply – just before the war it must have been – to oratorio, which I knew perfectly well was not a dramatic form, at any rate in the sense of things actually happening on the stage. I talked to Eliot about the idea and he was going to write the text for me. I hadn't by then thought I would ever do a libretto of my own.

PC: Was Eliot much involved with music?

MT: Music was his second interest. I asked him why he had called the *Four Quartets* that, and he said it was because the late chamber music of Beethoven was the sort of thing that he valued most, and that if he wanted to stimulate his own art he always went to music. I went to him, eventually, and said could he do the text for this particular oratorio. And he simply said, oh all right, but you must do the homework, you must tell me how many words you want, and what kind of words, and lay it all out in a plan. Eliot eventually sent for me and said, 'I've read it all and you'd better get on with it yourself.' He made the lovely remark: 'Anything I add to it will stand out a mile as so much better poetry.' But his whole advice was, 'Don't let the poets loose on your librettos, on anything, because they are going to do with the words what your music should do.' He said you should use absolutely known words, like the Bible, all extremely simple.

PC: Had Eliot given much thought to the problem of words working together with music?

MT: No, I should doubt it. You see I went to him to learn, and I was able to translate from what he as a master had to say about verse drama. I didn't want to hear what he thought about Verdi, or the texts of Verdi, because I could find that out for myself.

Eliot stood for a certain set of aesthetics, as you can read in the *Selected Essays*. His whole aesthetic interested me because it was a part of the classical movement against the romantic world. I came into a period when the choices were between expressionism, à la Schoenberg, or neoclassicism, à la Stravinsky. Those really were the two divisions and you went one way or the other. I wasn't so conscious of it then as I am now, and I couldn't have formulated it as I do now, but I was moving away very strongly from the romanticism of my predecessors. I didn't get anything from either Elgar or Vaughan Williams, except that I couldn't go that way; and so I was in a kind of neoclassicism and this meant years and years of struggle with the question of classic form. Eliot was in the same boat. He made the sort of remark which got me round the corners. [Despite our classical ideals], we were nevertheless in a romantic period, which he defined in a special way. He simply said that the material we were dealing with was black material, which kept oozing out of the contours we gave it – as he considered it did in *Hamlet*, and as he considered it did in the Shakespeare sonnets, where the material was not eaten up completely by the form. The ideal, as we talked of it, was when this black material could be wrestled

with and somehow contoured. This sort of insight was immensely valuable
for me.

The more interesting figures to me personally, the people I feel I belong
to, are figures in which both elements, the highly imaginative world and
the formal world, are always interlocking. That would be Yeats, where
everything is wrought out of a mixture of things, for example. Or Turner.

PC: And would you say that Eliot belongs to that number?

MT: Oh yes, of course.

PT: Did you want your own operas to grapple with black material?

MT: In my own operas the black material is probably in *The Knot Garden*,
and certainly hardly in *The Midsummer Marriage*. No, I think we're
generalizing it far too much; I never could think of opera as a generalized
thing, but only as a certain genre. When I finally got to the point of being
driven by something into the material of *The Midsummer Marriage*, then
in a sense this was not black material but material which was going to
be quite difficult to contour and put into a shape. But I knew its genre
and its tradition, you see, whether in Shakespeare or whether in music.
The question isn't any longer whether an opera has got black material,
or whether it's classical or unclassical, it's what will do this particular
job. And the job here was to break open the very classical works that I
had done, like the First Symphony and the Concerto for Double String
Orchestra, and move to the possibility of a huge lyrical expression.

The techniques of music weren't a problem at all, though I wasn't a
harmonist – I didn't know what harmony was. I couldn't have harmonized
Stainer hymns … to sound like Stainer. But I tried very hard, and very
early on I got hold of a German edition of Schoenberg's *Harmonielehre*.
And I just spat it out. I mean all I came to was pages and pages of all the
possible chords in fourths. The attitude was very German – that you can
have a chord by itself. But I knew perfectly well that no chord appears by
itself. It's part of a whole. I never think – I can't think – in chords, you see,
so that that was no good. It seemed to be balls. Then I went to Hindemith
and his *Unterweisung im Tonsatz*. Equally mad.

PC: How did you get on with writing the words for the *Child*?

MT: The text of the *Child* got printed by a boys' school somewhere down
in south London where they had a whole set of Gill Sans type, and it was
quite beautiful, the text done as it stands now, page by page, very tiny, very
nicely done. And one of these texts went, or I may have sent it, to the then
music critic of *The Times*. He wrote back in distress and said, 'Oh dear,
oh dear, how can you possibly be going to use this tiny lapidaric short text

for the purpose of writing an oratorio?' To which I wrote a nice splendid postcard saying, 'I would just like you to remember that the longest piece of choral music goes to the word "Amen".' He did not know his job. None of them did. But Eliot did.

He knew exactly the difference between a coloratura aria on a single vowel and a piece of narration. I cannot tell you how abysmally ignorant they seemed to me. They really did – quite desperately so. I used to go and talk to Eliot at Faber's in the afternoon sometimes, and at that period he was concerned with the question of verse poetry, and the nature of theatre, and of verse in the theatre. Which is all entirely analogous to the problem of music.

PC: To return to *The Midsummer Marriage*, how does it relate to *A Child of Our Time*?

MT: It came out of the oratorio, one sentence in which is a sort of attempted affirmation: 'I would know my shadow and my light, so shall I at last be whole.' Now I wanted to put that upon the stage. And bit by bit the accretionary process began, which is for me very long. An immense amount of material was collected up before we began to try to pare it away and make something of it. It was then that I reopened *Opera and Drama* and discovered that Wagner had had the same problems with a work like *Tristan*. And what does he do? He reads an enormous story which goes on for hours and hours, and by a tremendous effort of his mind it is reduced into three acts where virtually nothing happens at all. And yet it is all there. He was my master in that sort of sense. Incidentally, I did try to find a librettist who could accept the material, but it did not work. So that I was driven into it in the end.

PC: The material in *Midsummer Marriage* is certainly amazingly complex. What strikes one in comparison with the *Child* is that the opera begins with great particularity – the boy and girl on the eve of their wedding – and then after the first act the conflict between their personalities is completely taken away from them and expressed through the Ritual Dances and other symbolic events, so much so that the two people are almost obliterated until their transfiguration as Shiva and Parvati near the very end. The recent production by the Welsh National Opera (1976, with John Treleaven as Mark and Jill Gomez as Jenifer) actually did obliterate them, so that they were not seen at all at the transfiguration.

MT: Yes, that's wrong, but I know what they were trying to do. But this is more or less what happens. That is part of the nature of that kind of genre, I should think. I don't think you can do it differently.

PC: It's hard to think offhand of anyone else who has written an opera in which the boy and girl, or whoever they are, have their destinies taken right away from them.

MT: I think the oddity of it is more that the opera came at the time it did. I'm now talking generally, but this was at the end of the war when the concentration camps were opened and people were beginning to scream and shriek, and Francis Bacon was doing these things. Then this extraordinary opera appeared, which is as it were joyful and life-giving and yet is not bland. I don't know how it happened, because I was very, very well aware of what the world was like. So it was something that just came; it is the only opera I know of from this period that attempts this particular thing. I couldn't do it now because the irony of the world has become so strong – in me, possibly in the world in general, I don't know. Yet the polarity between *The Midsummer Marriage* and its time was sharper than ever, perhaps. But you want to look at the present day: the ironies have taken over, whether it's brilliant and funny like Stoppard, or whether it's harsh and black like Auden. The other isn't there. We've moved into an endlessly more and more ironic world.

PC: Were you ever tempted to ask Auden to write words for you?

MT: No, Auden wanted me to ask him, and that's another matter. Because, as you know, he thought of himself as the librettist of the age, and he had very strong views as to what [that role] should be. I go rather along with Eliot, who thought that [with *The Rake's Progress*] Auden had played Stravinsky a '*tour de passe-passe*' [sleight of hand], as Eliot himself described it. The librettos that he produced for Henze are simply such verbiage that I can't deal with them. I'm not given that way. I want an extremely good lapidaric style.

PC: What about Auden's famous remark that opera in the twentieth century has become the last refuge of the High Style?

MT: I don't make anything of it: that's Auden. I'm not writing in the 'High Style', and that's not the last virtue, so I'm out of it. And I don't feel that opera is directed to the High Style; I mean I'm not going that way, and *The Knot Garden* is not about the High Style. God alone knows what the final answer is – I've no idea. I come out from underneath the Auden net because I'm moving into a different world.

PC: How did the informal lessons with Eliot help with your operas? For if you're a poet, if you write verse drama, it would appear to be essential that every word should register, whereas I believe that you hold that in opera the only thing that really matters is that the situation is plain for all to understand.

MT: Eliot said to me that when he was writing the choruses for the women in *Murder in the Cathedral* he only expected one word to be heard per line. That's a remarkable statement by a poet. He discusses that question for himself in the essay on the three uses of poetry. If you read the relevant part of that essay and simply put opera for verse, or musical verse, you'll find it an absolute description of a libretto. Eliot said that there are three kinds of operations on the stage: stage drama, ballet and opera. And that there are three means of expression – music, gesture, and words, one of which was always on top, though all three were always there. In the drama proper, then, the words are on top, music is next and the gesture's at the bottom. You can do it for yourself: in the ballet, gesture's at the top, music next, the story's at the bottom. In opera, music gets on top, words are next and the gesture's at the bottom. That's very Eliot, but it taught me all I wanted to know – once I accepted it, you see, then I got the whole thing clear.

Susanne Langer somewhere makes the remark that if a song in a Shakespeare play were performed so well that you said, 'Oh that's a marvellous young man or young woman singing there – I wish they'd do a recital', then it's gone wrong. The music would be eating up the drama, whereas the drama must eat up the music. I thought that this would enable me to tell when operas had gone wrong, that is when the words begin to dominate. Incidentally, this is what I think is fascinating about Stoppard's plays: they sail close to all these techniques but the big moments are verbal, not musical. Therefore they aren't opera.

PC: The debate about words and music has gone on ever since opera began and it was, of course, one which much exercised Wagner. Did any of his theorizing about opera as a grand unity of all the arts make any impression on you?

MT: No, not at all. But I wanted something that Wagner had invented, and that was the ability to fill an empty stage with music. This was something which Schiller had wanted and didn't get, but Wagner did. This did interest me, so when I wanted to do it to open the second act of *Midsummer Marriage*, I knew I could. I had to produce a sound which would fill the stage with sunlight – stage sunlight, not real sunlight. And I could also risk having an ending where there was no one on the stage at all. You don't get that in Mozart, you don't get it in Beethoven, though you might get it in Weber, but hardly.

*   *   *

PC: How did you come from *The Midsummer Marriage*, where the sources for the story are relatively unfamiliar, to your second opera, *King Priam*, which recasts one of the world's oldest and most familiar epics?

MT: I think the first part of it was the feeling which other people had rather strongly, namely that *The Midsummer Marriage* had difficulties because it was material which you described as unfamiliar. It hadn't got a story line or whatever. And I was allowing myself to be convinced, though I don't think that their judgement was in fact sensible, because *The Midsummer Marriage* has now become so straightforward and clear to all the younger people. Once having been delivered in this way I began to consider the matter, and I suppose I'd known about the Greek world for years and years, in a sense. The *Priam* material interested me enough to feel that out of this amalgam I would move into that tradition of genre of the tragic world without becoming Verdi-ish – up to a point. But I'm not sure, because it's going to appear among the four operas as the one that is odd, because it's not an invented story. Though when you look at it, so much of all the other stories is taken from various bits of tradition: there's nothing invented at all.

I didn't go back and reread the *Iliad*. But certain things began to fall into place. What I was really concerned with was the birth-to-death story. The fundamental thing was that this was a shift of genre, a shift towards the possibility of a tragic hero. I came across a book called *Le Dieu caché* by Lucien Goldmann, who felt that under both Christianity and Marxism there could be no possibility of a tragic hero because everything was going to come out all right; either you went to heaven, or you had a Marxist heaven.

And I got annoyed by this in a way. I knew I was going to move away from that gorgeous sort of lyrical orchestral sound, with the voices riding on this sound, to something which was tougher, and where the English language would if possible be heroic, and voices would be able to sound heroic as they sang. This meant on one side the break-up of the orchestra. I had to refine what I wanted into a different kind of sound and then consider how small the number of instruments against which one voice could sing could actually be. There are places in *Priam* where the voice is only singing against a single oboe. So that was a big change.

The lyric arias disappeared because you were not in that situation, but there were what you might call monologues, which brought it close to Shakespearean things of another kind. That was one side. The other was I suppose the material itself, about which I went and talked to Günther Rennert in Germany.

PC: In the *Iliad* itself the action is very largely controlled from Olympus or wherever. The gods interfere to wrap people up in mists when they're in danger on the battlefield, or alternatively deprive them of natural protection. But in your opera the action is centred much more in the characters themselves – you give the power of choice to them.

MT: Yes, and that was partly under the influence of another book, whose title I've forgotten now, which was concerned with the notion that all drama has to do with the family. At the same time I was concerned with whether you could still put the supernatural on the stage, as I knew Eliot himself was with the Eumenides in *The Family Reunion*. Racine of course deliberately gave up this sort of thing because he thought that the Greek gods were evil and that therefore he couldn't put them on to the stage any more.

PC: That whole framework of beliefs was very different from ours, so in what sense did you think that the Greek gods might be put on the stage?

MT: We haven't any framework; we're in a period when you can get it from anywhere if you want it. But we've no real feelings of belief. We are in a world of finding something which we can no longer discover in the heavens. I think you can get a frisson but that's about as far as you can get. I don't go very far down this road in *Priam* because it is not about that to that degree really, except perhaps for the god Hermes who appears, but already the irony is beginning to be absolute. There is very little irony in Madam Sosostris in *The Midsummer Marriage*, she really is what she appears to be. Though there's a touch of irony in that she isn't there in the end, and nothing's inside her veils, as it were.

Incidentally, the whole operation of this long aria is taken straight out of a marvellous poem by Valéry called 'La Pithie' about a woman describing the loss of her womanhood and her becoming a seer. But by the time you get to Hermes the irony is very strong because he says straight out that he's a 'Divine go-between, that's who I am', and this upset some critics quite a lot. He's half divine and half undivine – just a throwaway character.

PC: Like Wagner's Loge?

MT: That's right, of course. But in the end he is allowed to sing 'An die Musik' [the aria 'O Divine Music'] and this is what his function *is*. This aria has been criticized quite rightly as regards the operatic structure because it delays the last scene. But I couldn't care less about that because that is what I have to say about what Music is.

PC: What was the impulse behind the score's amazingly bony, condensed and much more Beethovenian idiom?

MT: I'd finished with lyrical expression and moved elsewhere, but I can't explain to you what the impulse was, except that it was all of a piece with the impulse to go into the classical world and to have heroic singing, and that this necessarily involved a very sharp change of style.

PC: I believe that it was at about this time that you studied Brecht's theories about epic theatre.

MT: At the time of *The Midsummer Marriage* I was convinced that Wagner had got it right in *Opera and Drama* when he said that you could no longer have the Shakespearean theatre with a great many scenes in each play. Brecht taught me that you could. Wagner's view was that epic material had to be made into single acts which were absolutely condensed. In *Tristan* he actually achieves this. This idea fascinated me because I'd got everything mixed up in my mind, one way and another, all the notions of [the action] happening on a single day and so forth. Almost as strong an influence as Brecht was television and film, where cutting rapidly from scene to scene is of the essence. But I didn't then know the extent to which lighting techniques were to bring this technique into the theatre, though I suppose I sensed that this was the way we were going to move.

In *Priam* I particularly didn't want the technique – as in *Wozzeck* or *The Turn of the Screw* – where the curtain goes down on a musical interlude. This was solved in the first instance in *Priam* by having tiny scenes which do it for you. As the end of the first scene approaches the three characters present become a commenting chorus; they come down in front of the audience and talk to you in what is very nearly a fast recitative. They say: 'Scene will change into scene before you; time rolling with each scene away' – and in Sam Wanamaker's production at Covent Garden this actually happened. So this established a technique by which the scenes were to be changed without any curtain going down at all. And yet they are in fact interludial.

Near the end of the whole opera, just before Hermes enters as messenger of death, there is an interlude, reminiscent of the famous one in *Wozzeck*, which consists of one long sound where the whole orchestra begins low down and goes right up to the top for the start of the penultimate scene. And this is when Priam is theoretically on the ground dead – I mean waiting – and in that interlude he turns into the total tragic character. That had to be done on an open stage and it went on for about a minute. By the time I reached *The Knot Garden* I was thinking that we could go faster still, and I wanted the time between scenes to be cut to the minimum. But you can't do it as you can on the films, because they do it electronically. So in *The Knot Garden* you are given a tiny bit of non-music which lasts for about a quarter of a minute.

PC: Non-music?

MT: Harry Birtwistle called it 'non-music' to me once – something in which you could go all sorts of ways. It simply says quite clearly in the score that in these tiny moments the scene is broken up and changed in whatever way you want to do it.

PC: In *The Midsummer Marriage* you sent really only one couple, Mark and Jenifer, in search of themselves and, as we've seen, once they have embarked, the journey itself is undertaken on their behalf by the Ritual Dances, the other characters, and, of course, most powerfully by the music. But in *The Knot Garden* you have an analyst, Mangus, as ringmaster and three couples who have to work everything out for themselves, person to person.

MT: Yes, because again the tradition is different. It is that of *Heartbreak House* or Chekhov's *Cherry Orchard*, with a small number of characters caught, so to speak . . . .

PC: Would it be fair to see the second act of *The Knot Garden* as like that state described by Jung where the personality has to endure being shattered in order that it may be rebuilt more strongly?

MT: Well, they live out their dreams, and the background to that is *A Sleep of Prisoners* of Christopher Fry, where the characters dream each other's dreams: a very weird play, which fascinates me. But here in *The Knot Garden* things come out, if you like, through the surrealist technique. Thea didn't really whip her husband, nor I suppose did Faber really kiss Dov. You see some of the unconscious things put forward and therefore it's nightmare. They've all gone into this nightmare, but technically it is a series of duets.

PC: If the second act is nightmare, how far may one see the first act as the realistic grey light of day?

MT: Up to a point. The first act is really very good because all the characters are presented to you with extraordinary speed. The whole act is under half an hour. It's fantastically fast, and at the end they are all screaming on to a blues. If you look at it technically it's all very carefully done – of course by that time I knew what I was up to.

PC: If each of these characters has a dream world, what is the analyst Mangus' dream world?

MT: The analyst's dream world is that he's Prospero and can put the world to rights. He says it straight off: 'So, if I dream / It's clear I'm Prospero: / Man of Power. / He put them all to rights.' But it's phoney. At the end he says – how does he put it? – 'Prospero's a fake, we all know that.' And then he says something much more serious: perhaps it's gone so far that 'the Island's due to sink into the sea'. He's learnt how fake he is.

PC: What kind of analyst is this who plays therapeutic games with his fellow house-guests?

MT: I don't know, perhaps you can ask R.D. Laing if you want to. Some people think I got it out of Laing. I never read any Laing, but the thought amuses me.

PC: Or Iris Murdoch?

MT: Oh yes, it's much more out of Iris Murdoch, but she doesn't go into such a deeper world. Mangus is an older figure and he is as lost as anyone, but nevertheless some therapy has happened. You see at the end people have slightly shifted; not all of them, and only slightly, because that seems to me where we are. The possibility of cure is one of these vain illusions. What Mangus says is very important, and that's why it had to be spoken, not sung. He says it's enough, we can't go [on] … in fact he breaks the amorists up and he says, this game is getting too complicated – in a moment we shall really end in murder. So he says stop it, virtually. And then he does what Prospero does, breaks his staff and drowns his book.

Another vital book behind it all is *Shakespeare and the Comedy of Forgiveness* [by R.G. Hunter] which is about a tradition that Shakespeare got hold of. It really came from Spanish plays, Renaissance plays, which were concerned with the Christian idea that you could have any amount of murder and God knows what going on on the stage as long as at the end you have Christian forgiveness. Prospero says, what shall I do with these characters?

And it is Ariel who says, were I human, I would forgive them. So it's Ariel who teaches Prospero how to be human, but in the end Prospero – as a god or whatever it is – produces the scene of forgiveness. Mangus says that the power is in the play: in other words if you play, as R.D. Laing would say, then your therapeutics operate through the play. Denise, the freedom fighter, says that power is in the will, which is what she believed up to the beginning of the third act. But Thea, the gardener, is quite different. She doesn't say anything – she simply steps across the circle and shrieks out forgiveness: 'Blood from my breast'. Now that comes out of one of the Spanish plays, where the mother produces blood from her breast as a sort of therapy. Absolutely real.

PC: Which play would that have been?

MT: I don't know, I can't remember anything of it: I never remember where I get anything from. You store these metaphors for your own purposes and they give you what you want. All I wanted is a tiny amount of possibility that, if you read it properly or listen to what the music says, she is shifting into forgiveness, which is the operative thing for me as it is for Shakespeare. The lovely aria she has finally when they've picked up the pieces of the chessboard, and she's left there on her own, is all about forgiveness. 'I hated him all day when I was in my garden, but now I know' – a very curious line – 'Nature is us.' You go into your garden but you only find yourself.

PC: There is no split between nature and culture.

MT: In her sense, no, because she has gone into her garden to find a method of getting away from the problems of the marriage. So she finds herself there, and that is how she comes out of it. Each of the characters comes a certain distance. You may feel that the next morning the married couple will fall out again apart on the wrong side of the bed, as Faber describes it. But it may not be so, because they have come together in this possibly deeper way. I had to find my own metaphors, and after a long, long problem they appeared and they were absolutely dead right.

For me, though I am not saying for somebody else, libretto writing is an assemblage of metaphors. I do not invent verbal metaphors, that is not my job; I invent musical metaphors, but verbal metaphors have necessarily to be part of it. In *The Knot Garden* it is very interlocked and intricate and quite successful. The new opera, *The Ice Break*, is not so successful because the problems are risked very sharply, as to how to use American slang and what it is and what its relations are. And there are practically no purple passages.

PC: The libretto seems extraordinarily fined down and concentrated, and in fact …

MT: Just as quick, incidentally. All the music is over in an hour and a half, so Colin Davis tells me. But that's a minor matter.

PC: One notices that the text carries a comparatively light frame of reference and cultural echo. It has a narrative immediacy and is almost Stravinskyan in its terse economy.

MT: Yes, surely.

PC: It also looks like a drama very much of the chorus rather than of individuals.

MT: Well, that's partly how it came about. I wanted to put the chorus back upon the stage. One of the things that set me off was seeing *Benvenuto Cellini* on the Covent Garden stage. I became fascinated with the anonymity of this chorus, thrashing about like crazy as it does in the carnival scene. I thought, my God, that is some part of the world. People go on, choruses rush around like crazy.

PC: But you'd already done that in *The Midsummer Marriage*.

MT: No, they don't really rush around at all. They're all there, almost entirely [still], watching what's going on. They go and play games sometimes, but you never see them doing it. In the new opera they are on some trip somewhere and quite dis-related, apparently, to the actions of the remaining main characters. I was also concerned – which may or may not come off – with the anonymity of the chorus, that it might be sort of stereotyped: we are all involved in stereotypes of one kind and another, including stereotypes of sex for that matter. Whether we can ever get out of it is, of course, an endless preoccupation as far as I am concerned: whether rebirth is a reality. … I mean how far we can present that on the stage. It is there in *The Knot Garden*, and probably in *The Midsummer Marriage* as well.

Here it's taken in a rather more visual sense, because the young man, Yuri, really is broken up and his bones smashed up, and he's like a large egg, sitting locked up in white plaster of Paris. That scene is from the end of *Back to Methuselah*. A huge egg is brought upon the stage and the egg rolls away, and the girl says I want to get out, I want to be let out. They break it open and she steps out and at once behaves like an adolescent and goes straight to the most good-looking man she can see. It's all very amusing and nonsense – typically Shavian. This always remained in my mind, this egg, but in the new opera of course it isn't really an egg, because it can't be, and also of course it's a rebirth, not a birth.

The new opera is about self-righteousness: when we are God and the others are the devil, or however we may put it. We are good and they are bad and must be eliminated to make the world right. That's in the brutal sense, for there's the possibility that these [positions] really are stereotypes. The black girl suddenly says, 'No I can't go that way', and then inquires of herself what it may be. She uses a marvellous metaphor, 'I scrabble for unformed letters / That might make a word'. That is as I see it where we are, even if the word will get broken up again almost immediately afterwards. We've no answer. But she knows, and all she says, from something murmuring inside her, is that you can't go and mince other people up. As a character she believes … in the quality of her own death, that something might come of it.

Yuri, the one other character who comes through in the opera, has a natural rebirth – he has to go through a traumatic death. He's anything but born into freedom, rather into the reverse. He has all the Turgenev fathers-and-sons complex, which is all mixed up in it. But in the end there is a vital reconciliation.

In the new opera a messenger comes – I daresay from the stars – but he's not going to let himself be turned into a god this time. He says, 'Who old me? You must be joking!' He's only a messenger, and only a psychedelic messenger at that.

PC: What about the musical style of *The Ice Break*? Are there jazz elements in it?

MT: No, none at all.

PC: Is it a development of the musical language you were using in *The Knot Garden* or …?

MT: Partially, but … I don't feel it that way. The change is in the chorus singing, which is much more like … a lot of slogan singing almost. There are no beautiful choruses like in *Midsummer Marriage*. They are not there at all. Nothing of this kind.

PC: Were you tempted to use any kind of familiar tunes, perhaps pop songs or whatever, as a basis for the slogan chanting?

MT: There's only one, and that's a hymn tune which was used by the Ku Klux Klan in the nineteenth century. Not that you would probably recognize it, or want to. They sang hymns when they collected each other to drink together. A man went round the villages on a horse, blowing a trumpet to summon them. This is all in the opera in point of fact, and you'll hear the trumpet. They didn't necessarily meet to mince somebody up, though they did occasionally do so of course, and then when they were there they sang a hymn, which was a Methodist hymn written by an American. Oddly enough, someone in Schott's [Tippett's publishers] knew the tune because he'd been brought up as a Methodist. This comes for a moment in the opera at an extremely slow pace. But it's not really what it's about. When the Klan danced there was a sort of surreal, barbaric dance, and one of the other tunes in the opera is a hoedown, which the Ku Klux Klan used to dance quite a lot.

PC: In their hoods and all?

MT: I can't tell you that. Yes, I should think so. They danced to a fiddler who was called Fiddling John Carson. There's a picture of them dancing to the fiddle with a man on the gibbet above them – I believe it was taken about 1913. This was not a black man, he was a white man, oddly enough. It had taken them two years to get him out of jail, and then they strung him up and danced below the gibbet to a fiddle.

PC: Are we going to see anything like this in *The Ice Break*?

MT: Yes, you'll see plenty of it. You'll see the fiddling: you won't see the gibbet.

Selected Writings

In the following list of the author's writings, * indicates that the item appears in this book. Where the title has been changed, the original is given in square brackets. UP = University Press.

1 Books

Faust as Musician: a Study of Thomas Mann's 'Doctor Faustus'
  (London: Chatto & Windus, 1973).
Wagner and the Art of the Theatre
  (New Haven and London: Yale UP, 2006).

2 Contributions to Books

'Bayreuth Festspielhaus', in: *Grand Opera: Story of the World's Leading Opera Houses*, ed. Anthony Gishford (London: Weidenfeld & Nicolson, 1972).
'The Staging of *Tristan and Isolde*: Landmarks along the Appian Way', in: *Tristan and Isolde*, English National Opera Guide, ed. Nicholas John (London: John Calder, 1981).
Preface and annotation to: *Thomas Mann: Pro and Contra Wagner*, ed. Erika Mann et al, trans. Allan Blunden (London: Faber, 1985).
'The Novella Transformed: Thomas Mann as Opera', in: *Death in Venice*, Cambridge Opera Handbook, ed. Donald Mitchell (Cambridge: Cambridge UP, 1987).
'Allegory: The Romantic Era; The 20th Century', in: *The New Grove Dictionary of Opera*, ed. Stanley Sadie (London: Macmillan, 1992).
'Designing Wagner: Deeds of Music Made Visible?', in: *Wagner in Performance*, ed. Barry Millington and Stewart Spencer (New Haven and London: Yale UP, 1992).
'Faust in his Element: a Musical Career and Its Consequences', in: *The Romantic Tradition: German Literature and Music in the Nineteenth Century*, ed. Gerald Chapple, Frederick Hall, Hans Schulte (Lanham, Maryland: UP of America, 1992).
'Stage History', in: *Richard Wagner: 'Die Meistersinger von Nürnberg'*, Cambridge Opera Handbook, ed. John Warrack (Cambridge: Cambridge UP, 1994).
'Landfall on the Stage: a Brief Production History', in: *Richard Wagner: 'Der fliegende Holländer'*, Cambridge Opera Handbook, ed. Thomas Grey (Cambridge: Cambridge UP, 2000).
* 'Reinventing Wagner after Hitler', in: *Mettere in scena Wagner*, ed. Marco
Targa and Marco Brighenti (Lucca: Libreria Musicale Italiana, 2019).

'Lighting the Way from Vienna to Bayreuth: *Tristan und Isolde*, 1903-1962', in:
    Wagner's'Tristan and Isolde' in 1903 Vienna: Context, Impact and Interpretation, ed. Anna
    Stoll Knecht and Anastasia Bellini (New York: Routledge, forthcoming).
'Historic Stagings (1876–1976', in: *Richard Wagner in Context*, ed. David Trippett
    (Cambridge: CUP, forthcoming).

3   Lectures and Contributions to Journals and Programme Books

'Opera as Mystery Play' (on Wieland Wagner), *Times Educational Supplement*, 27 September
    1968.
'Wonderful Bayreuth *Tristan*' (on a revival of Wieland Wagner's 1962 production), *The Times*,
    20 August 1969.
'Herr Wagner Deprecates Theories' (interview with Wolfgang Wagner), *The Times*, 5
    September 1969.
'Wagner on a Disc' (on Wolfgang Wagner's 1970 *Ring* production), *New Statesman*, 28 August
    1970.
'With Helmet, Shield and Spear?' (review of: Detta and Michael Petzet, *Die Richard Wagner-
    Bühne König Ludwigs II.*: München, Bayreuth), *Times Literary Supplement*, 20 November
    1970.
'Tannhäuser – Enemy of the State' (on Götz Friedrich's 1972 Bayreuth production), *Times
    Educational Supplement*, 15 September 1972.
'Wagner and the Idea of the Song Contest', Bayreuth Festival programme, 1973.
'Squaring the *Ring*' (on Götz Friedrich's Covent Garden *Ring* production), *Times Literary
    Supplement*, 11 October 1974.
'Thomas Mann and the Ghost of Old Klingsor', *Cambridge Review*, 30 May 1975.
'Wagner for Perfect Sceptics' (on the Boulez/Chéreau Bayreuth centenary Ring, 1976), *Times
    Educational Supplement*, 3 September 1976.
* 'Damming the Rhine', *Times Literary Supplement*, 10 June 1977.
* 'Michael Tippett on Opera' ['The Composer as Librettist: a Conversation between Sir
    Michael Tippett and Patrick Carnegy'], *Times Literary Supplement*, 8 July 1977.
'Straightening Out the Cycle' (on the Solti/Hall Bayreuth *Ring*, 1983),*Times Literary
    Supplement*, 26 August 1983.
* 'Klemperer: Sufferings and Greatness' ['The Irreproachable Daemon': 'Beethoven's
    Beethoven'], *Times Literary Supplement*, (in two parts) 6 April 1984 and 13 September
    1996.
'Street Scenes from World History' (on the Barenboim/Kupfer Bayreuth
Ring, 1988), *Times Educational Supplement*, 2 September 1988.
* 'Solti: Still Climbing the Mountain' ['Making Music that Breathes'], *Times Literary
    Supplement*, 2 January 1998.
* 'A Touch of Wagnermania', *Wagner News*, April 1998.
120 articles and reviews as Stratford-upon-Avon theatre critic for *The Spectator*, 1998-2013.
* 'Karajan: The Conductor as Supreme Being' ['The Conductor as Supreme Being'], *Times
    Literary Supplement*, 20 November 1998.
'In Search of the Magic Mountain: Letter from Davos', *Times Literary Supplement*, 4
    February 2000.
* 'Phantom at the Royal Opera' ['How Long before Ofop Steps in?'], *London Review of Books*,
    16 March 2000.
'Which Way to the Grail?', The Royal Opera programme (*Parsifal*), 2001, pp. 42-9.

* 'Toscanini: Champion of the Divine Art' ['Champion of the Divine Art'], *Times Literary Supplement*, 10 May 2002.

'Swan's Way: a Brief Stage History', The Royal Opera programme (*Lohengrin*), 2003, pp. 37-44.

'Reflections on "a Vulgar Theatrical Career"', The Royal Opera programme (*Die Walküre*), 2005, pp. 38-42.

* 'Blood on the Carpet: English National Opera in Retrospect'['Blood on the Carpet'], *Times Literary Supplement*, 1 January 2010.

*'Wagner's Shakespeare', lecture first given at Trinity Hall, Cambridge, 2013. ('Wagner and his Shakespeare', chapter one in this book, is an expanded version of this lecture.)

*'Designs on the *Ring*' (on the artist Josef Hoffmann), *The Wagner Journal*, July 2010.

* 'Reckoning up the Ring' (on Alfred Pringsheim's 1876 Bayreuth diary), *The Wagner Journal*, July 2014.

'Syberberg's *Parsifal* and the Soul of Germany', *The Wagner Journal*, July 2017.

* '*Tristan und Isolde*, Vienna 1903', lecture given at Jesus College, Oxford, 2018.

Index

Illustration Credits

Grateful acknowledgement is made to the following sources. Unlisted illustrations are from the author's collection, from other private collections or from sources it has not been possible to trace.

Bayreuth: Richard-Wagner-Museum 40, 47 (Ill 3), 48, 53 (Ill 7), 87 (Ill 2), 90 (Ill 7) Bildarchiv Bayreuther Festspiele 47 (Ill 2), 76, 88, 90 (Ill 8), 91 (Ills 10, 11, 12), 93 (Ills 16, 17), 94 (Ills 18, 19) Nationalarchiv der Richard-Wagner-Stiftung 14, 15, 18, 26, 87 (Ill 3)
Bayreuth: Archiv Bernd Mayer 85
Berlin: Staatliche Museen zu Berlin, Preußischer Kulturbesitz, Kunstbibliotek 23, 24, 60 (Ill 2) Ullstein Bilderdienst112
Berne: Collection suisse du théâtre 69, 89, 91 (Ill 9)
Dresden: Joachim Herz Privatsammlung 33, 92 (Ills 13,14,15)
Herrenchiemsee: König Ludwig II Museum 61
Leipzig: Staatgeschichtliches Museum 20 (Ill 8), 25
London: Decca/World Orchestra for Peace 127 (photo Terry O'Neill, courtesy Charles Kaye)
London: Clive Barda 132, 139
London: National Portrait Gallery 145
Munich: Hans-Jürgen Syberberg Privatsammlung 97, 98
Munich: Deutsches Theatermuseum 16: photos by Siegfried Lauterwasser, jacket, 30, 31, 34
New York: New York Times 106
Triebschen: Richard Wagner Museum 30
Vienna: Österreichiches Theatermuseum 62 (Ill 5), 62 (Ill 7), 64, 65 (Ills 9, 10), 66 (Ills 11, 12), 68, 73, 75 (Ills 18, 19) Österreichische Nationalbibliotek Bildarchiv 44, 50, 59, 60 (Ill 3), 67 (Ills 13, 14) Universitätsbibliothek 49
Worms: Cornelia von Bodenhausen Privatsammlung 53 (Ill 8), 54
Zürich: Thomas-Mann-Archiv der ETH 37, 42

Every effort has been made to contact copyright holders, but if there are any inadvertent omissions or mistakes the author and publisher will be glad to correct them at the earliest opportunity.